WHAT'S
SHAKIN'
YOUR
LADDER?

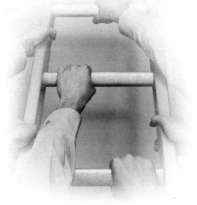

Tues meeting. { Chy + Prayer
                 Hospital

Wed night -   Scott
              Parenting
              diversity

Penny +

WHAT'S SHAKIN' YOUR LADDER?

15 CHALLENGES *ALL* LEADERS FACE

Samuel R. Chand

Mall Publishing, Co.
THE PRINTED WORD THE PLANTED SEED
NILES, ILLINOIS

Printed in the United States of America

Published by:
Mall Publishing Company
5731 West Howard Street
Niles, Illinois 60714
877.203.2453

Book Design by Marlon B. Villadiego
Cover Design by Andrew Ostrowski

ISBN 0-9760362-1-5

Scripture references are from the following versions:

KJV: King James Version.

MSG: Scripture quotations from THE MESSAGE. Copyright © by Eugene H. Peterson 1993, 1994, 1995, 1996, 2000, 2001, 2002. Used by permission of NavPress Publishing Group.

NIV: Scripture quotations are taken from the *Holy Bible, New International Version*®. NIV®. Copyright © 1973, 1978, 1984 by International Bible Society. Used by permission of Zondervan. All rights reserved.

For licensing / copyright information, for additional copies or for use in specialized settings contact:

Dr. Samuel R. Chand

P.O. Box 18145
Atlanta, GA 30316
404-672-2681 x108
www.samchand.com
samuel.chand@beulah.org

Table of Contents

Introduction: **What's Shakin' Your Ladder?**

The California mudslides of 2005 washed away homes, cars, and roads. In one case, a large boulder rolled loose, blocking the highway. Cars were stuck on both

> If handled successfully, what is it that could move you to where God has called you to be?

sides of the rock, which created an insurmountable obstacle for drivers. The next day, a photo of this rock in newspapers around the country illustrated the problems better than any article could. It showed the frustration of motorists who were not prepared for the rain and consequently were trapped by their circumstances.

What's Blocking **You?**

Is there one big rock in your life? A roadblock to leadership? What is blocking you from your destiny waiting on the other side? Let me ask the question another way. What is your biggest leadership challenge? If handled successfully, what is it that could move you to where God has called you to be?

What is the big rock in the middle of your highway?

When I consult with church leaders or business executives, I've found the same challenges are common to all leaders. Regardless of whether you are leading a small church or a Fortune 500 company, there are fifteen common challenges all leaders share. We're going to look at each one in detail.

As president of Beulah Heights Bible College, I tackled these same fifteen challenges. Each time I confronted them I thought, *I am the only one who has ever had to face this before.* But now as a leadership consultant, I talk to thousands of leaders each year; and I've learned that leaders have more in common than we have separating us.

Leaders need to know that they're not the only ones who are

Challenges Common to All Leaders

1. Focus: Finding and maintaining what is important.
2. Vision Casting: Learning how to cast vision in a way that causes people to respond.
3. Communication: Saying it in a way that everyone gets it.
4. Decision Making: Understanding how we make decisions, so we can make them better.
5. Choosing the Team: Making critical decisions as to who is on our team.
6. Leadership Development: Growing our self and others.
7. Change vs. Transition: Intentionally planning transitions for smoother change.
8. Conflict: Understanding the importance of health during conflict.
9. Organizational Congruence: Aligning formal and informal structures with the vision.
10. Financial Management: Seeking advice from knowledgeable counselors.
11. Time Allocation: Distributing the resource of time effectively.
12. Control vs. Delegation: Learning when to hang on and when to let go.
13. Execution: Getting the job done.
14. Future Thinking: Focusing on what comes next.
15. Legacy: Passing our values on to future generations.

facing these hurdles. We can learn to recognize patterns of failure and success from those who've faced similar circumstances. These challenges aren't a phase we go through once and never return. We don't learn how to handle a challenge once and then never face it again. Instead, we will continue to face the same obstacles throughout our personal and professional lives.

Think about it. How many of us have said, "If I could just get organized?" The implicit thought is that if we do it once we will never have to do it again. That's not true. We may temporarily control the clutter; but as we take on additional responsibility, additional clutter comes with it. Whether that clutter is in our office (additional paperwork), our time (additional meetings), or our mind (lack of focus), the challenge will continue to reoccur.

The fifteen challenges presented in this book are not like a rock in the middle of the highway that we go around once and never come back to. If we're having problems dealing with a two-million-dollar-budget, imagine what it will be like to manage a fifty-million-dollar-budget. If we have challenges with a staff of five, think about the challenges we'll have with a staff of 157. No, these challenges aren't rocks we go around; these are challenges that will continue to rock our world.

The Ladder **Analogy**

In my third book, *Who's Holding Your Ladder: Selecting Your Leaders—Leadership's Most Critical Decision,* I developed an analogy with a ladder. The ladder represents a vision. The ladder climber is the leader who pursues that vision, but he or she can't do it alone. To climb to the top of that ladder, the leader must have someone holding the ladder. So the focus of the book is on dealing with staff and organizational issues.

Many readers found that analogy helpful so I continued it in my fourth book, *Who Moved Your Ladder?: Your Next Bold Move.* In it, I discussed personal transition issues such as how to respond when God starts to transition us from one place (ladder) to another or from one vision to another.

Using the rock analogy is helpful to some because they can focus on what is blocking them, but it doesn't help us understand the ongoing nature of these challenges. That's why I extend the analogy in this book. The title helps remind us that the challenges we face aren't something we deal with once and then never have to worry about again. Instead, the higher we go on the ladder, the more the reverberations of these challenges will shake the ladder from the bottom to the top.

As leaders, it is our job to learn how to hold on to the ladder even when it is being shaken. It is also our responsibility as leaders to figure out how we can prevent or minimize shaking in the future. Can we reduce the reverberations? Can we stop the top of the ladder from swaying? Can we secure the bottom better?

Understanding these challenges will help us to secure our foundations. The challenges will continually shake our ladders, but we can learn how to hang on while it sways, anticipate when it is coming our way, and keep it from shaking all day.

Teaching Points

Following each challenge in the book, the "Teaching Points" section provides a short review of the chapter and practical suggestions on how to prevent and stop this particular challenge from shaking your ladder. After reading the book, I encourage you to use this section as an outline for teaching the material in this book to others in your organization so they can also learn how to handle these challenges successfully.

CHAPTER ONE

FOCUS

Focus is reflected in the capacity to identify and devote the majority of your time and energy to the "critical few" objectives and issues, while still managing to deal with the "important many."

—Sam T. Manoogian, independent leadership consultant

P astor Walker looks out the window of his office, wondering what to do next. Last night a respected deacon presented an idea for a new evangelism program designed to reach out to businesses and homes near the new church building. This morning the music minister wanted to discuss adding a worship service with a different type of music to attract new people to the church. Each idea could obviously reach new people.

But in order to finish the new sanctuary on time, Pastor Walker had to address the growing pile of construction-related paperwork on his desk. As he shuffled through the documents, he saw a business card and remembered the conversation with the man who gave it to him. A well-known Christian evangelist with a national speaking ministry was looking to expand. He had asked Pastor Walker to join him as a guest speaker at his conferences. It was a flattering offer, but was now the time to pursue it? As he looked at the opportunities and decisions before him, Pastor Walker felt overwhelmed.

As leaders, we often have so many opportunities before us that it's hard to focus on only one. This dilemma isn't unique to pastors or churches. Business leaders also face the same struggle when adding new products and services, changing their marketing approach, or evaluating opportunities to expand. When presented with overwhelming choices, how do we focus on the "critical few" while still managing to deal with the "important many"?

Finding Focus Is Not Difficult; **Keeping Focus Is**

Pastor Walker's building plans should be his primary focus; and it is likely he knows that but is distracted. If there is a marriage retreat going on at his church, that's good; but that's not his focus. If the deacon has a great idea about outreach, that's nice; but it still isn't his focus. If the music minister wants to start a second service, that's exciting; but it isn't his focus either. The new building is his priority; it is his rock in the middle

> When presented with overwhelming choices, how do we focus on the "critical few" while still managing to deal with the "important many"?

of the highway. When the new building is completed, Pastor Walker can have a bigger marriage retreat, more outreach opportunities, and new services. Without completing the sanctuary, these programs won't reach their full potential because he will always be distracted by construction issues.

As president of Beulah Heights Bible College, people always wanted to give me a new focus. They would come to me with additional course ideas or new directions for the school to pursue.

"You need to offer a major in this field."

"You know there's a real need in the marketplace for this service."

"If you had this event, I know we could have a great response."

Employees, customers, and church members have their own agendas for us, making focus the biggest challenge we face at every level of leadership. While their ideas may be worthy of consideration, they can distract us from our mission. Each morning we come to the office with a plan, but if we're not careful, our plans get shifted by the plans of others. Our calendar will get filled. We should be the one to fill it.

We've all had days when we didn't feel like we accomplished anything. We feel like a Ferrari driving through a school zone; we can't give

> **Focus is the biggest challenge we face at every level of leadership.**

it our full power. We've given 10 percent to this project and 12 percent to that project, but we haven't pushed the gas pedal all the way down on one project. How can we ever accomplish anything this way?

Satan may never tempt us to rob a bank, sniff cocaine, or cheat on a spouse. If he can keep us from accomplishing anything, he doesn't have to. Rather than knock us out of our jobs through sin, he

> **What Satan can't pollute, he will dilute.**

can keep us in our jobs doing nothing. We can stay and be ineffectual, and he wins. What he can't pollute, he will dilute.

Growth Multiplies **Our Distractions**

As our organizations grow, there will always be more to distract us. When we start a new church, all we want to do is get a few people to work alongside us to provide a great worship experience. We're not worried about office space, land acquisition, PA systems, or payroll benefits. We've got a single focus: We want to find five people who are breathing and willing to help.

Five people soon grow to fifteen people. As the number of people increases, the work environment becomes more important. No longer can they work out of borrowed space, they need an office of their own. So now we've got *people* and *place* as our focus. As the staff increases to twenty-five or thirty people, we've got to have programs in place. Managing those *programs* requires systems and *procedures*. Suddenly, the focus isn't only on people. Now we have to consider people, places, programs, and procedures. Our focus gets diluted.

Then people inside and outside of the organization want to know how we're planning to grow. Now we've got to have *plans*. When there were only five people, our only plan was to get three of them together at the same time. That's not enough anymore. Now we've got to have a plan for today and five years from now. When we started, we didn't even have a bank account; now we've got accounting issues, payroll deductions, and tax reporting. And it never ends. What started as a single focus has now become a smorgasbord of attention-demanding focus stealers.

> As we grow, we get distracted by the increasing needs of the 5Ps: people, place, programs, procedures, and plans.

If we look around at our growing organization and see that the people are confused, before blaming them we need to stop and ask, "How focused am I?" When we get out of focus, our people are unsure how to respond and unable to move forward.

Other signs of being distracted include the following:

1. Getting Marginalized. Marginalization happens when our input and influence is reduced or limited to only a few areas. Decisions are made without our input or we attend meetings to vote on an issue; and it doesn't matter because the votes needed have already been decided.

2. *Being Diverted*. When nonessential things occupy our time and thoughts or when resources are used for things that aren't necessary, we've lost focus. If Pastor Walker spends his time picking out songs for the new worship service rather than finishing paperwork related to the construction of the new building, he's diverted from the important to the trivial.

3. *Getting Attacked*. Resistance and overt attacks can remove our focus from the main issues. As I said earlier, it may not be a headlining sin that Satan uses to attack us; it might be a whole lot of small distractions.

4. *Getting Seduced*. When pleasing our allies becomes more important than staying on a difficult course, we're definitely distracted. If Pastor Walker is afraid of upsetting the deacon's feelings and instead encourages him to move forward with the project, the pastor is being seduced by a need to be liked.

We know that keeping focus is hard. You may even find it hard to continue reading because of all the distractions you're facing right now. But if you stop reading every time your cell phone rings, an e-mail comes in, or your favorite television program comes on, you'll never get to the solutions you are hoping to find. Keeping focus is difficult even when you know what it is.

> **Keeping focus is difficult even when you know what it is.**

The Meaning of **Focus**

So what exactly is focus, and how do we keep it?

Pastor Scott Wilson of Oaks Fellowship Church in Red Oak, Texas, and I were talking about focus when Pastor Scott gave me a great insight. He told me that while he was praying, the Lord helped him to understand the meaning of focus. Here's what he said:

F = First things first

O = Other things second

C = Cut out the unimportant

U = Unify behind vision

S = Stick with it

Isn't that a great definition? Focus means putting the important things first and leaving everything else for second. If we can cut out the unimportant and unify behind the vision, we'll always have focus. Of course, the most important thing is sticking with it. Pastor Scott's definition is practical. It systematically tells us how to have and maintain focus.

> As leaders, we're used to multitasking and are proud of it, so we inadvertently encourage it in the people who work for us.

But to have focus in our church or business, not only do *we* have to be focused, but so does everyone who works with us. We have to teach them to be focused as soon as we hire or recruit them.

Most leaders can do eight things at once and do them all well. But sometimes we mistakenly have the same expectations for the people who work for us. Perhaps I hire Bob to be the new accountant. After he starts work, I learn he is also a gifted Web designer. I've needed an updated Web site for some time, so I ask Bob to see what he can do to improve the company's site.

As the others in my organization learn that Bob is updating the Web site, they want additional information or pictures added to their pages too. Soon he is spending more time updating the company Web site than he is processing the payroll.

As leaders, we're used to multitasking and are proud of it, so we inadvertently encourage it in the people who work for us. We even say things like, "Around here, everybody wears five hats." While it is true that there are times in an organization's history and growth where everyone needs to step up and wear as many as fifteen hats, as the organization grows we've got to bring in people who are focused. In Bob's case, I've essentially encouraged him to abandon his accounting focus. What happens at our next meeting when someone asks to see the financial report?

Bob says, "I didn't do it because I was updating our Internet presence."

Do I want to step up and say, "Oh, by the way, thank you for funding this new accounting position we needed so badly; but I've got him doing something else right now"?

No, I hired him to be an accountant because I needed an accountant; and I need Bob to do that job. The fact that he is filling other

The main thing often becomes the thing that is most neglected

roles is because I didn't clearly define his focus. The other people at the meeting won't judge Bob by his Web abilities; they'll only judge him by his accounting performance.

Often we hire someone and say, "Thirty percent of the time you will be doing this, and seventy percent of the time you will be doing that." It sounds good and may even look good on paper, but the main thing often becomes the thing that is most neglected. Ultimately, it won't be the employee's fault; it will be the fault of the leader who didn't keep her focused. As a leader, we must help those around us to understand and stick to their focus.

And we must stick to ours. Sometimes we're tempted to help our people do their jobs, rather than lead them. We know we're gravitating toward doing the work, rather than leading, when we make these types of statements:

"Here, I can do that for you."

"I'll help you finish that, I've done one like it before."

"Let's sit down and go over all the things you need for the project."

"Yeah, we did that program at my last church. Let me get some stuff out of my files for you."

If everyone in the organization, including the leader, wears only one hat, then we can ask for and get higher levels of accountability and performance. Our focus should be on leading people to the right hats and helping them keep it on their heads.

Focus Comes from **the Who**

How do we find our focus? Pastor Scott's definition gives us some practical tips for keeping focus, but what if we don't know what it is? Maybe we think that grabbing a legal pad and making a list of the things we need to do can determine our focus. We take the list of eighteen or 118 jobs and try to combine items to make big rocks out of all of our little rocks. Then we prioritize those rocks and pick one rock as our focus for the day. We think that making a list will bring about focus. But the to-do list only shows us *what* we're focusing on. *What we focus on should always flow from who we are.*

> The starting place for finding focus should always be with questions like: Who am I? If I were to die today, what would I most regret leaving unfinished?

excellent The starting place for finding focus should always be with questions like: Who am I? If I were to die today, what would I most regret leaving unfinished?

Once we define *who* we are, then we can do the *what* because the (*what* has to flow out of our *who*.) This is true for our entire organization because the organization is a reflection of the leader's vision, or the leader's *who*. How we accomplish our vision is *what* we do. Our organization can't do the what until it understands the *who*.

(Church programs should be the result of our vision for the

church) If a program doesn't fit our vision, we shouldn't be doing it. It doesn't mean it's a bad program; it only means that it isn't for our church at this time.

I had a conversation with Bishop Eddie L. Long about this subject several years ago. Bishop Long leads a large church of 25,000 members in Atlanta, and together we spent hours trying to figure out what his vision was. Finally, we came up

> As we get older, there's something within us that says, "I want to give more time to less things."

with FLY, which stands for Family, Leadership, and Youth. Once Bishop Long was able to articulate his vision—his personal focus—he was able to move anything that had to do with FLY to the top of his list. If it didn't fall under the FLY vision, that didn't mean it never got done; it only meant that it wasn't a priority for him and his church at this time. Since his focus is so clear, Bishop Long is able to allocate money and time to programs that fall under the FLY vision. Without guilt, he can also say no to things that distract him from this vision.

It is important to find our focus, but we also need to know that at different times in our lives, our focus will change. As we get older, there's something within us that says, "I want to give more time to less things." Our focus will narrow even further. Perhaps Bishop Long will feel a need to focus on training leaders, or perhaps he will focus only on youth. Maybe it will be something else entirely. But regardless of *what* he does, it will always come out of *who* he is.

Focus Needs to **Be Communicated**

Once we know what our focus is, we need to communicate it throughout our organization. We'll cover this process in detail in the next chapter on casting our vision, but there are a couple of points that should be made here. First, the actual process of succinctly communicating vision can help us sharpen our focus. We need to be able to communicate it in small sound bytes. If we can't condense the vision to something that fits on a T-shirt, are we really that focused? Or could we further refine the focus? Second, our people are more likely to work toward our vision if they are clear on what it is.

Many people go to work to do a job. They learn specific things like how to use software or how to build a truck. But when we take time to teach people *why* they are doing *what* they are doing, we help them to have a deeper understanding of their focus. Suddenly, they aren't only building trucks; they're creating reliable transportation for people who deliver food to families via the supermarket. No longer are they entering names into a software database. Instead, they are making sure that visitors to the church will be promptly ministered to. By sharing who we are and how what they do relates to our vision, we teach them that who they are is also important.

Getting people to think at this level will increase the dialogue about focus within the organization. If we invite honest and open conversations, we may find that the people around us start asking difficult and probing questions. At first this may make us uncomfortable, but we shouldn't feel threatened. Questions are signs that they are thinking at an organizational level. This kind of dialogue can help our people to make better decisions and use their time and resources more wisely.

If Pastor Walker doesn't know what to do next, imagine how confused his people must feel. Our focus is our light. Diffused, it can still brighten a room. But when concentrated, focused into a laser beam, there is not a more powerful leadership tool.

Teaching Points

1. Finding focus is not difficult; keeping focus is.
2. Focus is the biggest challenge we face at every level of leadership.
3. What Satan can't pollute, he will dilute.
4. Growth multiplies our distractions.
5. Signs of being distracted include:
   - Getting marginalized.
   - Being diverted.
   - Getting attacked.
   - Getting seduced.
6. Pastor Scott Wilson's definition of focus is:
   F = First things first
   O = Other things second
   C = Cut out the unimportant
   U = Unify behind vision
   S = Stick with it
7. We have to teach our people to be focused as soon as we hire or recruit them.
8. Multitasking employees may look good on paper, but ultimately they will lose focus. The main task they were hired for will become the most neglected one.
9. Be a leader, and avoid the temptation of helping others to do their jobs.
10. If everyone wears only one hat, we can ask for and get higher levels of accountability and performance.
11. Focus isn't found on a legal pad of things we need to do.
12. The starting place for finding focus should be with the questions: Who am I? and If I were to die today, what would I most regret leaving unfinished?
13. Once we define who we are, then we can do the what. The what has to flow out of our who.

14. At different times in our lives, our focus will change.
15. Continually communicate the focus throughout the organization.
16. Don't be threatened by people asking questions about focus.
17. Focus needs to be a laser beam of light.

CHAPTER TWO

VISION CASTING

The very essence of leadership is that you have to have vision. You can't blow an uncertain trumpet.

—Theodore Hesburgh, former president of Notre Dame
University for 35 years

I am not a fishermen. Yet each July I find myself on a boat hoping to catch something, maybe a small fish, a large boot, or even a cold, so I don't have to embarrass myself any further.

Four other people and I serve on the board of a church in Las Vegas. None of us are members or even live in the city; we are brought in as business counselors for the operation of the church. Each year we attend a retreat in Missoula, Montana where we all climb into boats, row out into Bitterroot River, and we fly-fish.

Fly-fishing is different from the drop-your-pole-in-the-lake kind of fishing that many are familiar with. In fly-fishing, the key is in the casting. The best rod and reel and the perfect bait won't help. Unless the fisherman knows how to cast, he's not going to catch anything.

The perfect cast involves both hands working at the same time, pulling and throwing simultaneously. I think. I actually don't know because I've never caught anything. The other people in my boat? They know how to cast. The proof is in the fish they catch.

Last July I grew increasingly frustrated as I watched another board member catch something every third cast. I cast and cast all day long, and I didn't catch anything. I did learn an important lesson. The power isn't in the number of times we cast; the power is in the perfect cast. This is also true of vision casting. We can have the perfect vision, but unless we know how to cast that vision, it will never grab hold of anyone.

> We can have the perfect vision, but unless we know how to cast that vision, it will never grab hold of anyone.

Leaders often think that vision casting is telling people the plan: "We're going to build a new multipurpose space." That isn't vision casting. It's an announcement about why parking will be disrupted. Vision casting is less like an announcement and more like a pitch the professionals use to entice potential investors. When business leaders want to expand, they have to find someone who will invest money in the business now with the hope of future rewards. For a business leader to hook an investor, she not only has to communicate the plan, but she has to sell the future benefits.

When we cast our vision, we must think of it in the same way. We are not trying to inform people; we are trying to get people to invest. To capture the imagination of those vision-investors, we need to have a strategic plan based on who we're trying to catch.

Five Types **of People**

Generally speaking, there are five different types of people we need to catch with our vision. Each of these types will respond to different kinds of bait and hooks. If we understand who we are trying to catch, our casting will be more successful.

Excited **Embracers**

These people are excited to embrace our vision. They are ahead of the curve and believe that whatever we're proposing is a good idea the minute we suggest it. They don't need to hear all the details. They will feed off our vision, multiply it, and bring it back to us

Excited Embracers	—	2 percent
Early Embracers	—	18 percent
Middlers	—	60 percent
Late Embracers	—	18 percent
Never Embracers	—	2 percent

with new ideas. They have energy, they're excited, and they're on top of things. Unfortunately, there are few of them. Excited Embracers make up approximately 2 percent of the population.

Early **Embracers**

Like the Excited Embracers, Early Embracers will embrace our vision early, though maybe not with as much zeal as the Excited Embracers. These people will stick with us as we work to make the vision a reality. Early Embracers make up approximately 18 percent of the population.

Middlers

Middlers are the largest group. They make up approximately 60 percent of the population. These people hear our vision and want more time to think about it. Even after they've considered what we've told them, they're still squarely in the middle. They're not against the vision, but neither are they for it. In fact, they probably won't make up their minds one way or another unless a friend convinces them to. In the 2004 presidential election between George Bush and John Kerry, analysts called these undecided Middlers the Swing Voters because they could swing their vote for either candidate.

Late **Embracers**

Unlike the Middlers, Late Embracers have already decided that they aren't in favor of whatever is on the table. However, late in the game, when there are no other choices left, they might grudgingly follow. They make up approximately 18 percent of the population.

Never **Embracers**

We can always count on Never Embracers to disagree, no matter what the subject is. Don't plan on trying to change their decisions because their minds are already set. Fortunately, they make up only 2 percent of the population.

As we prepare to cast our vision, we know that the top 20 percent are strongly behind us, no questions asked. The bottom 20 percent are against us and asking a lot of questions. So as we get ready to cast the vision, we need to target the Middlers, the 60 percent who have not yet made up their minds.

Unfortunately, what most leaders do is ignore the top 80 percent and immediately try to pacify the bottom 20 percent. We say things like, "If I could just get that 20 percent over here with me." But we already know they are negative, pessimistic, sticks-in-the-mud, who aren't going anywhere. Yet we keep going back to these same people. We bring new bait, we get a better rod and reel, and we continue to frame our vision in such a way that we hope to catch their imaginations. But no matter how many times we cast to the Late and Never Embracers, we rarely catch those fish.

Let's say that I am driving to the church for a meeting with five people. Of the five, Andrew, Beverly, Cynthia, and Darius are all positive people. Gerald, on the other hand, is annoyingly negative. He repeatedly asks the same questions, he can't track the vision, and

Take the bottom 20 percent and ignore them.

he won't get with the program. The other four are on board, they get it, and they are ready to go. But during the drive, as I think about my presentation, who am I thinking about? I am thinking about Gerald. As I mentally rehearse my presentation, I think about Gerald. Then I begin to take a God-sized idea and whittle it down to an Gerald-sized one, hoping maybe he will buy into it.

I have a radical suggestion. This is contrary to what we've *amen* been doing, and it will take some getting used to; but it works. Take the bottom 20 percent, the ones we've been focusing all of our attention on, and ignore them.

That's right. Don't pay any attention to them. They aren't going anywhere, and they're not going to help us no matter what we do. So rather than focus on them, do the opposite and ignore them.

Of course, we'll want to treat them like we treat the other groups. Make sure they get the same information, they're notified of the same meetings, and they hear the same God-sized vision everyone else hears. But don't do anything special for them; they get what everyone else gets. We don't set up special meetings, we don't take them out to lunch, and we don't change our presentations in a way that will appeal to them alone. We no longer cater to them. As a population, we should treat them like we treat anyone else.

The first thing we notice is that we have more time. No longer are we setting up special meetings, revising our presentations, or worrying about the Late and Never Embracers. When we stop making special accommodations for people who aren't about to change their minds, we have more time and energy.

Now take this newfound cache of time and spend it on the top 20 percent. Hanging out with the Excited and Early Embracers will pump them up. Listening to their ideas and encouraging them into leadership roles will empower them. Suddenly, they become our allies in an intentional way.

> **Informal influence works best with Middlers.**

As soon as there is momentum in the top 20 percent, we need to swing our attention to the large percentage of people in the middle. Just as candidates energize their bases and then go after the undecided votes, we can direct our attention to the Middlers after we've excited the base.

The mind set of Middlers is different than that of Embracers. The top 20 percent come to meetings to get excited. The bottom 20 percent come to meetings to get mad. The Middlers? They don't come to meetings. If we call a special meeting to cast our vision, the Middlers won't be attending.

Middlers also tend to resist authority and authority figures. They are more easily influenced by their peers and colleagues than they are by authority. Informal influence works best with Middlers. These are the people the candidate shakes hands with in the diner or the candidate's wife meets at school. Embracers, on the other hand, are the ones who show up at televised town-hall meetings, waving signs.

When we're casting vision, how do we reach Middlers? We reach them informally. Instead of inviting them to special meetings, we talk to them in hallways, restrooms, and parking lots. We meet them over a cup of coffee, we share a pizza, or we discuss the vision while stacking chairs after a fellowship meal. Middlers will be much more receptive to our vision in these informal settings.

Casting the **Big Vision**

When God gives us a vision—a really big vision—such as a renewed focus on global missions, a new community outreach program or a new building, we need to be strategic about how we cast it. I recommend taking a copy of the employee or church directory and dividing each person into one of the five groups discussed earlier. Individually consider whether she is in the top 20 percent, the bottom 20 percent, or right in the middle. We need to know who we are going to spend time with and who we are going to ignore.

Then we should meet with the top 20 percent and show them the list of Middlers. Ask the Excited and Early Embracers, "Who do you know on this list? Are any of them your friends?"

Allen might say, "I am friends with the Smiths, the Johnsons, and the Harveys."

Then ask Allen to talk with them. Allen should be the one to communicate the vision, and he can do so informally since he is already friends with them.

Repeat this process for everyone who is in the top 20 percent. Let them pick out their friends and casually talk to them about the vision. Essentially, we are unleashing the top 20 percent to deal with the middle 60 percent. We're not asking the top 20 percent to change anyone's mind or say anything they're uncomfortable with. We're asking them to have honest dialogue with people who haven't made up their minds in hope that we can get them off the fence. They should just talk about things they already believe. For example, "I'm excited about the building program Pastor Archie is talking about. Finally, we're going to have a home of our own. Aren't you excited about it too?"

Middlers change their minds by osmosis, so if a friend tells them how excited they are, Middlers will say to themselves, "Maybe I ought to get excited about this too." And that's how it happens.

Most of us cast our best pearls in front of the bottom 20 percent. But Scripture warns against casting "your pearls before swine" (Matthew 7:6, KJV). I am not calling a group of people names, but I think this situation is a good application of that particular verse. Swine will trample our pearls and then turn on us, making us look like we're the bad guys. If the same Scripture were written in a modern translation for leaders, it might say, "Don't cast your vision in front of the bottom 20 percent because they're going to destroy your vision and turn on you."

This is an example of how we can be strategic in our casting. We have to prepare our message for the people, but we have to know what type of person we're going to be talking to. We want to spend most of our time with the people who want to see our vision fulfilled. Then we can make them messengers to their friends, so we aren't the only vision communicators.

It's Never **the Meeting**

Always remember this: The meeting is never the most important thing. The meeting before *the meeting* and the meeting after the meeting are more important than the meeting. So in my example of five board members where Gerald was the negative one, I would meet with each of them privately. I would

> The meeting before the meeting and the meeting after the meeting are more important than the meeting.

personally share my vision with Andrew, Beverly, Cynthia, and Darius at a meeting before the meeting. But I would also meet with Gerald before the meeting. That way he doesn't feel like I never talked with him. But when I meet with him I won't empower him or cater to him.

When it comes time for the actual meeting and we are all together, I will say things like: "It's been such a delight talking to all five of you about my vision, and it is wonderful to see how everyone has responded. I have talked with each of you, and I am so encouraged about the feedback each of you has given me." So I never give power to Gerald. I don't point out in the middle of the meeting that he is the only one who is against it.

After I've made my initial comments, then I start with the most positive person and say, "Andrew, tell us what you're feeling about this." Then I let Andrew pump everyone up. I will go around the

> There are some people we just have to let go.

table doing this from the most positive to the least positive and will leave Gerald as the last guy. It becomes a kind of peer pressure. The Excited and Early Embracers will move the Middlers to their position and the Late and Never Embracers move toward the middle because they don't want to be left out.

I've done this enough times that I've seen it work. Even if Gerald remains glued to his position and only makes negative comments and even if he does it for months and months of meetings, pretty soon it becomes clear to everyone else that Gerald is just negative. Eventually Gerald will start to say things like, "Looks like I'm the only one who keeps saying these kinds of things." Exactly. But in the meantime, the work keeps getting done; and I didn't have to point Gerald out to the group. He revealed himself.

That's why the meeting before the meeting and the meeting after the meeting are the most critical meetings we have. It is never the meeting. If we haven't made strategic decisions and done our homework on the people before the meeting, we aren't ready to cast our vision.

Finally, there are some people we just have to let go. These people aren't unique to one organization. They are at Beulah Heights Bible College, IBM, and The Coca-Cola Company. We might know them from our neighborhood association, Sunday

School class, or kids' school. They're everywhere. So this is not a church thing. This is just a human thing. Not only will these people not invest in our vision, but often they won't invest in anyone's vision. But that's okay. Once we understand the group dynamics of how to influence people and bring about change, we can move forward with the 80 percent who are behind us.

Vision Is **Top Down**

I hate it when I call a business and have to be transferred five or six times to get the person I need. Some doctor's offices are like this. The patient leaves a message with the scheduler if she wants an appointment. She calls one nurse if she wants to talk to the doctor, a different nurse if she needs a prescription refill, and a third nurse to get her test results. Even though there is only one patient and one doctor, it seems that multiple departments have created their own territories, and they can't help her unless it is in their area.

> There can only be one vision and one visionary in the house.

Some churches are like this. They've got a men's thing and a women's thing. These are separate from the Christian education thing. The children's thing is different than the youth thing; and, of course, the family thing is a whole other thing.

There can only be one vision and one visionary in the house. The vision needs to come from the top down. We can't have every department in a business or church casting its own vision; otherwise we will have what Bill Hybels calls "a federation of sub-ministries." Leaders must wait for the leaders above them to cast their vision first.

In one of my seminars a woman I'll call Gloria described the difficulty she had trying to make changes to the women's ministry at her church. She wanted the women to meet more frequently, reach out to hurting people in specific ways, and generally to move beyond the socials and fellowship they now enjoyed. However, when she tried to cast this vision, it hit the floor with a thud.

At this church, the pastor had already cast his vision. He wanted the church to be a hospital for sick and hurting people. When the women heard Gloria's vision for the women's ministry, they were confused and overwhelmed by all the changes. I recommended that at the next meeting, the pastor remind the women of his vision for the church. After that, he could introduce Gloria and describe how the two of them had agreed on Gloria's plans to implement his vision into the women's ministry by reaching out to hurting people.

This time, when Gloria gets up and says, "Our church's vision is to reach out to others in need. We need to do more than just fellowship, we need to meet more frequently, and we need to reach out to others," her ideas will align with the church's vision. And the women will be more receptive.

Notice I suggested two things here. I suggested that the pastor first cast the vision to the church at large, which in this case he had already done. Then it makes sense for the pastor to pass the vision onto his leaders, so they can take it to their people. My recommendation was that the pastor stand in front of all the women and tee up the ball for Gloria to take a swing. Without this kind of top-down vision planning and execution, anyone in the organization can have a vision and be casting it everywhere, resulting in a mess.

A great example of top-down vision casting is found in Joshua 1. In this chapter, God speaks to Joshua, giving him a vision. Joshua then takes that vision and speaks to the leaders. The leaders speak to the people, and the people respond back to Joshua. We can all learn from this powerful example.

Vision Casting Must **Be a Priority**

In every service, in every meeting, it doesn't matter where we are or who we are talking to, we need to find a way to work the vision statement into the conversation. We don't have to quote it verbatim each time unless it's a catchy slogan, but we do have to keep the message and the essence of our vision in front of our people at all times.

We need to teach them to be vision-centric. Say to them, "This is our vision. Now the church down the road to the left is doing this, and the church down the road to the right is doing that, and that is wonderful for them. But our vision is different. This is our vision." That vision should then drive all of the budgeting, staffing, and programming issues at the church. This is what makes a vision-centric church.

If Gloria's church has a vision to be a spiritual hospital, the largest percentage of their spending should go to ministering to sick and hurting people. The church may not have a ministry for young mothers, but they probably have a well-thought out plan on how to care for the sick and dying. They may not spend a lot of money bringing in special musicians; instead, they spend that money on recovery programs. See how being vision centric actually drives the decision making within the church?

The same is true for businesses. If I have a small interior decorating business and my vision is to give the customer the house of her dreams on a small budget, I don't spend much time shopping for lamps at Tiffany's. In fact, I probably spend more time getting to know the customer than I do shopping, so I can be sure I am giving her what she wants. Likewise, an interior decorator who focuses on providing unique heirloom pieces probably spends more time shopping for antiques than she does in her customers' homes. In each case, the business is vision-centric. The vision actually drives the decision making.

Out of **Alignment**

What happens when the vision of the leader is different than the vision of the people? Maybe my staff has a different focus. Maybe the church I lead wants to go in a new direction. The first question I should be asking is: How did this happen? The second question is: How did this happen on my watch?

Leaders must accept responsibility for what goes on in the organization. If there is a split in the vision of the church or business, the leader must answer the questions as to how this happened and how it happened now. Then the leader must figure out what to do to change it.

If my church moves away from my vision, I can't jerk them back with one sermon or one staff meeting. Instead, I need to think of myself as an orthodontist trying to straighten teeth. I need to put the braces on the teeth and then with each visit I must slowly turn the key to bring the teeth back into alignment. I can't just tighten them in one motion and say, "You've got straight teeth now." Doing that could cause damage, and the results won't last. Likewise, I need to tighten and turn my people a little at a time until I bring them back to the vision.

I don't want to beat people up or accuse them of not doing what they should. It is not their fault that the vision went the other way. It is the leader's responsibility. Many leaders in this situation will say, "I had no choice." But we do have a choice. We always have a choice. When we say we don't, we give up our ability to do anything to change the situation. Taking responsibility for a wandering vision will gain us an opportunity to correct it.

When I talk to the staff of an organization, in only a few minutes I can see who has and who hasn't bought into the leader's vision. If the people say, "Pastor's vision is ..." instead of saying, "Our vision is ..." there is a disconnect. If the leader says something like, "My people really want to do this and they want to do that," his language reveals that he hasn't bought into their ideas. The words used can alert us to vision that has shifted between the leader and his people.

Benefits of **Shared Vision**

The name *Ritz-Carlton* evokes thoughts of superior service and luxurious pampering. This association isn't by accident. Ritz-Carlton managers train every employee to live by the company Credo. The Credo begins with this sentence, "The Ritz-Carlton Hotel is a place where the genuine care and comfort of our guests is our highest mission." The Credo continues with a pledge to the guest of "the finest personal service and facilities," "a warm, relaxed yet refined ambiance," and a promise to fulfill "even the unexpressed wishes and needs of our guests."[1]

Imagine living up to that vision! No wonder every employee is trained on the twenty Ritz-Carlton basics. The first basic is: "The Credo ... must be known, owned and energized by all."[2] Not only do they have a vision, but the first thing everyone who works for Ritz-Carlton must do is memorize, own, and live out that vision. Imagine how our business or church could grow if everyone knew, owned, and energized our corporate vision.

But this isn't a business-only concept. The Bible talks about the effectiveness of people all working together toward the same vision in Genesis 11. The people of Babel came together to build a tower that reached to the heavens. They used brick instead of stone and they used tar for mortar. Not only did they agree on the vision, but they also agreed on the tactics to fulfill that vision. Those of us who've worked with a neighborhood association on adding a new fence or changing the landscaping of our property know how hard it is to find agreement on construction details. To see the people of Babel agree not only on the design but the methods of building is quite an accomplishment!

> *But the LORD came down to see the city and the tower that the men were building. The LORD said, "If as one people speaking the same language they have begun to do this, then nothing they plan to do will be impossible for them" (Genesis 11:5-6, NIV).*

There is an important lesson in these verses. Not only does the vision have to be cast—and cast correctly—it has to remain in front of the people until they absorb it as their own. The words used are important. Previously I used the example of "My people have a vision ..." and "The pastor has a vision ..." to illustrate how language is used in a church where the vision isn't shared. Now Genesis gives us an example that anything can be accomplished when everyone is using the same language.

The goal of a leader is to cast the vision out to the people and hear it returned in these words, "Our vision is...." When the vision is properly cast, nothing is impossible for us or our organization.

Not even fly-fishing.

Teaching Points

1. Casting vision is less like announcing and more like recruiting.
2. Be strategic when casting vision.
3. Segment people according to these five categories:

   - Excited Embracers — 2 percent
   - Early Embracers — 18 percent
   - Middlers — 60 percent
   - Late Embracers — 18 percent
   - Never Embracers — 2 percent

4. Spend time recruiting the top 20 percent to interact informally with the Middlers.
5. Ignore the bottom 20 percent. Don't do anything special, but

keep them in the same communication loop as everyone else.

6. Remember the meeting is never what is important. It is the meeting before the meeting and the meeting after the meeting that make the difference.

7. Vision must be cast from the top leader down through the organization.

8. Continue to keep the vision in front of the people by teaching them to be vision-centric.

9. When the vision gets out of alignment, take responsibility. Correct it slowly.

10. With shared vision, anything is possible.

Notes

1 www.ritzcarlton.com/corporate/about_us/gold_standards.asp#credo
2 Ibid.

CHAPTER THREE

COMMUNICATION

*The leader has to be practical and a realist, yet must
talk the language of the visionary and the idealist.*

—Eric Hoffer, an American philosopher

"She just doesn't get it!" I fumed in frustration.

Julie is bright, articulate, and educated. Her work in the educational community is well recognized. So why can't she understand what we're trying to do in our church? *Maybe I need to explain it to her again,* I thought. *Maybe I can help her to see the real issue.*

However, subsequent meetings failed to enlighten Julie; and my frustration grew, turning into resentment. I began to question her spiritual status. Obviously, anyone who was right with the Lord would be able to see what he was doing at our church, I reasoned. I knew I had gone too far, but what else was I supposed to think? Why is it that someone like Julie, a good person with good credentials, just didn't get it?

Communication **Styles**

Thinkers come in two kinds: concrete or abstract. Their communication style follows their preferred way of thinking. Leaders are generally abstract thinkers. They talk in vague platitudes. They are great visionaries. But followers or doers are generally concrete thinkers. When they talk, they use specific, concrete terms. The difference in the communication styles between leaders and followers can lead to confusion.

If a pastor says, "We want to reach our community for Jesus," that is an abstract sentence. There is nothing tangible about it. We can't measure it, we can't feel it, and we don't know if or when we've accomplished it. This kind of statement will drive concrete thinkers crazy.

Immediately they will pepper the pastor with questions: "So how are we going to do that?" "Is that a one-mile radius or a two-mile radius?" "Are we going to go out two by two, or in threes?" "Are we going to have training?" "If Sue is doing the training, I am going to take it, but I hope they have it on Tuesdays. I can't go on Mondays because I have to take my kid to basketball practice."

The pastor didn't say anything about radiuses, going out in pairs, training, or even Monday's training class. But as concrete thinkers, they've already begun to apply the specifics to an abstract comment.

Now as leaders, this is where we often mess up. We don't consider how our abstract messages will be received by the concrete thinkers in our congregations. We just throw it out without any regard to how they will hear it. So we get up front and say, "Today I am going to cast a vision and then next Sunday I am going to come back and tell you how we're going to fulfill that vision and give you the details of our strategy."

This is a bad idea.

When concrete thinkers don't have enough information, they take what they hear and fill in the details. Then they pour mental concrete, the quick-set kind, on top of it. The following Sunday, we will have to blast their concrete thinking out of the water in order to lay the foundation we want laid. Essentially, we come back to them and ask them to

> **The biggest change we will ever ask anyone to make is to change his or her mind.**

change their minds. The biggest change we will ever ask anyone to make is to change his or her mind. Why do we want to do that?

Leaders who are abstract thinkers need to become concrete communicators. We need to provide our own details when we cast the vision. A better idea is to say, "We're going to reach our community for Jesus, and we're going to do it from 10th Street to Hallgate and from Hallgate to Division. We're going to give you training to help you do this, and the training is going to be every Monday night for the next six weeks."

My Challenge

This allows us to pour our own concrete. We get to quickly set the vision the way we want it set. I've messed up enough times on this to know the consequences of not doing it, and I've seen what happens when leaders do it right. When communicating vision, we need to be the one who sets it in concrete.

Every January there are pastors in pulpits all across America casting their visions. Then they give their people a whole week to figure it out. That's too much time for church folk. That gives them 168 hours to do a lot of damage and send a lot of phone calls and e-mail. They will spend that time guessing and second-guessing the vision.

It also happens in businesses. When the president of the company says that there will be a major reorganization without providing any details of what that reorganization looks like, some of the best employees will be at their desks looking for new jobs because they think it means they're being fired.

31

As leaders we can be both concrete and abstract; but our followers or employees may only think concretely. We can broadcast in both AM and FM, but they can only hear AM. We have to make sure we broadcast the vision in a way the receiver can hear it. To do this, we need to give our people the abstract and the concrete at the same time.

> As leaders we can be both concrete and abstract; but our followers or employees may only think concretely.

Bad Communication **Habits**

Communicating only when we need something. We can't be the kind of bosses who only speak to employees when we need something. No employee wants to feel like he or she is only there to serve the boss. As leaders, we need to be conscious of how we treat the people around us. Larry Bossidy, chairman of Honeywell International, a $24 billion dollar corporation said, "If you don't have the interest and the energy to get to know your people and your business, you won't be successful."[1]

Bossidy is right. It does take energy to be interested in people, but the truth is the energy we spend getting to know our people will be multiplied in their productivity. What employee wouldn't want to go the extra mile for a leader who truly cares about him?

Not following-up. The best-laid plans will never do more than gather dust unless we actually do something to implement them. In Chapter 13, I will talk about the poor execution of vision that challenges so many of us; but I want to point out that poor implementation and lack of execution is often made worse

> The biggest gap in American leadership right now is the gap between what is said and what is done.

because of our sloppy communication patterns.

Bossidy wrote a book with Ram Charan and Charles Burck, *Execution: The Discipline of Getting Things Done.* In it

Who does what by when?

they propose that the biggest gap in American leadership right now is the gap between what is said and what is done, in other words, a lack of follow-through.

To see more work completed we need to hold people accountable. We can do this by ending our meetings, e-mails, and conversations with a few key questions:

so imp

- What is the next step?
- When will it be completed?
- By whom?

A little bit of follow-through each time we communicate will result in a whole lot of execution.

Not returning phone calls or e-mail. Many people lie on their answering machines. "Please leave a message, and I will get back with you."

Instead, it should say, "Just leave a message, and if I feel like it, I will call you back. If I don't call you back, it means I didn't want to talk to you; so just chill."

Not only is it plain courteous to respond to someone, not responding allows others to pour the concrete. If they can't get an answer from me, they will get an answer somewhere else; and it may not be the answer I want them to have. Here's what I do when I don't have time to give them a full answer. Perhaps I get an e-mail with eighteen questions I can't answer, I respond as soon as I open it and say, "I will read it and respond to you in a few days."

Even though I can't answer all of their questions immediately, they aren't left to wonder whether or not I got the e-mail. They receive a reply and know that I am on top of it. We all know how frustrating it is to send something and never hear back. We can't follow through with people if we don't talk to them in the first place.

Lack of basic courtesy. I hope I don't even have to say this; but when communicating with people, use basic courtesy. Say please and thank you. We do it when we go through the drive-through at McDonald's. "Could I have a number three combo, please? Thank you." Why can't we do it with our coworkers? Sometimes when people work in close proximity, they forget the small niceties:

"Will you please do this?"

"Thank you for the report."

"You're welcome."

"My pleasure."

"Anytime."

Think how the atmosphere around the office could change if everybody used basic courtesy.

Focusing on the negative. Some people have a gift for grabbing the negativity in any situation and holding on. The most important thing a leader does for his people is to push back their horizons and put blue-sky thinking into their lives. We need to pull the positive out and add value to it rather than focusing on what was going wrong. When someone starts out, "Every year that I've worked here, something's gone wrong," gently try to help him see the other side.

> Most malpractice suits against doctors could have been averted if the doctor had just listened.

"I know this is a big deal, and things seem to keep happening; but think of all the other things you've overcome in the past few years. A year from now this will be only one more thing added to that list. You've been able to work through all of those issues; I think you can work through this one too." Help put some BS (blue sky) into their thinking!

Not Listening. When people talk about communication, they usually talk about sending the message; they rarely talk about listening to it. But for any message to be effective, someone must receive it. If we're not listening to the people around us, we're not good communicators. Hearing what someone else says not only helps us to understand what he says, but it helps us to know how to respond to him as well. The consequences of not listening can be severe. *The New England Journal of Medicine* has published studies showing that most malpractice suits against doctors could have been averted if the doctor had just listened.

Like doctors, those of us who are leaders are in the answer-giving business. When we are in answer-giving mode, it is hard for us to listen. But listening is an art we can cultivate. Active listening includes observing body language and making eye contact with the person we are with. It is how we sit when we deliver a message and how we respond to questions.

Listening and **Answering**

Now what does *listening* have to do with *answering* questions?

By really listening, we can hear the question the person is asking. Sometimes people don't ask the question they really want answered. For example, if a mother of a young child says, "Is the planning meeting *really at 5:00* today?" she may be wanting more than a confirmation of the time and place. She may be thinking, "How late is that meeting going to go because I have to pick up my child at the

> The question behind the question is the real question.

babysitter's?" If we answer her question with a "yes," we won't have really answered her question. She will continue to be frustrated that she can't be in two places at one time.

Instead, if we observe her body language and listen to the

way she phrases the question, we can respond differently, "Something seems to be bothering you." Then she can tell us that she has to pick up her child, that the presentation won't be ready in time, or that she was hoping to get approval on the plans before noon. A "yes," while technically correct, may cause us to miss information that she wouldn't volunteer without a little coaxing. We wouldn't even know to prompt her for more information unless we heard what she was trying to say without words. Remember the first question presented is never the real question. The question behind the question is the real question.

Often people ask me a question; and after I respond, they say, "The reason I asked is because … ." That's the real issue. The opening question merely begins the dialogue.

Listening is more important than speaking. Close observation and thoughtful responses can help people know that we hear what they are really trying to say. By paying attention to others when we communicate, we'll always be able to give the right answer, even when we don't have one.

An Example of a **Great Communicator**

To learn from the greatest communicator, the only one who ever communicated perfectly, we can read the New Testament and study Jesus. He could give a graduate seminar on communicating. When he spoke, crowds gathered to hear what he had to say. When asked a question, he didn't always answer the question that was on a person's lips; he answered the question in his heart. After studying the Gospels, I think the most instructive passage on communication is also the first example of Jesus being at the center of a crowd:

> And it came to pass, that after three days they found
> him in the temple, sitting in the midst of the doctors, both
> hearing them, and asking them questions. And all that

heard him were astonished at his understanding and answers (Luke 2:46-47, KJV).

In this example, Jesus is only twelve years old. Mary and Joseph have started the long walk back home after the Passover holiday not yet realizing that Jesus isn't with them. He stayed at the Temple to talk with the doctors and rabbis who met there regularly for debate and discussion.

> Jesus was there to hear them and ask questions, which led to understanding and his ability to give answers.

Four things are important to learn from this passage. What was Jesus doing in the midst of the doctors? Well, the passage says that he was hearing them and asking questions. Those are the first two important things: *hearing* and *asking questions.*

This led him to understanding, and then he was able to give them answers. *Understanding* and *answers* are the third and fourth things to notice in this example. Jesus was there to hear them and ask questions, which led to understanding and his ability to give answers.

Think about the sociological context of this period. In the Judean culture, women and children had no place with these rabbis who were sitting around stroking their long beards. So how did Jesus earn the right to sit in the middle and hold court? What allowed him this special treatment? To the community at large, Jesus was nothing more than Mary and Joseph's son; and, frankly, those rabbis probably didn't even know or care who Joseph was, let alone know his son. What gave Jesus his entrée to this elite crowd?

I can tell you what his entrée was. As those rabbis and doctors met and discussed these deep issues, this little twelve-year-old kid named Jesus stood on the edge of their great theological debate and listened. The longer he listened, the more he heard. After awhile I imagine there was a pause in the conversation; and

Jesus spoke up and said something like, "Rabbi Moshi, could I ask you a question, sir?"

Indulging the child who had been listening for so long, they allowed him a single question. But when he asked the question, it revealed such deep insight and power that the scholars were soon asking themselves, "Where did that question come from? Boy, that's a deep question for a twelve-year-old." And with his insightful question, he had earned the right to an answer. So they answered him. Then he asked another penetrating question, and then another, and that continued until Jesus understood their position.

Soon they wanted to know more about what he thought. The conversation changed course, and they began to ask him questions. Then he was ready with the answers; and the discussion continued until three days had passed and his parents came back to collect him.

Jesus was holding court with these learned men, but the situation didn't start that way. It started with him listening, observing, and hearing what *they* had to say.

What do we typically do when we come across a discussion? Many of us jump right to the answer giving. We miss some of the best opportunities to communicate because everywhere we go, we talk. We never go simply to listen. When there are three or four people in the hallway, we never stand there and become part of the group; we want to be the one who gives the answers.

As leaders, we need to do more listening. We need to resist being the one who knows it all. By listening to others, we learn how to communicate more effectively with both abstract and concrete communicators. We receive better information from those around us, and then we gain a greater understanding of the situation. If our conversations turn to conflict they will occupy too much of our thinking. Here are some actions I learned to do when communicating with people like Julie:

- Try to empathetically understand her concern.
- Realistically determine if she is a *won't* or a *can't*. A won't is about attitude; a can't is about ability. Both can be helped, but in different ways.
- Don't attach spiritual issues to a lack of response.
- Make sure I am broadcasting on her frequency.
- Remember it is my responsibility as a leader to communicate effectively.

The most important conversations are always going to be the ones we have with ourselves. The conversations in my head regarding Julie were filled with anger, doubt, and frustration. Stopping to listen to what I was telling myself, as well as taking a communication time-out to reassess the situation, showed me that I needed to be the first to change.

Learning to listen to others and to our own self-talk will help us respond appropriately, even to the Julies who frustrate us.

Teaching Points

1. There are two kinds of thinkers and communicators. People are either concrete or abstract.
2. Leaders are generally abstract thinkers; they are great visionaries and talk in vague platitudes.
3. Doers or followers are generally concrete thinkers. They use specific, concrete terms.
4. Concrete thinkers fill in their own details when they don't have enough information.
5. Leaders who are abstract thinkers need to become concrete communicators.
6. Communicate vision so that all receivers can hear it. To do so, give the abstract and concrete at the same time.
7. Avoid these bad communication habits:
   - Communicating only when something is needed.
   - Not following up.
   - Not returning phone calls or e-mail.

- Lack of basic courtesy.
- Focusing on the negative.
- Not listening.

8. To get more done, follow up all communications with these questions:
   - What is the next step?
   - When will it be completed?
   - By whom?

9. The first question isn't the real question. The second question is the one people really want answered.

10. Listening is more important than speaking. Observe body language.

11. Jesus is the only example of a perfect communicator. Here's what he did in the order he did it:
    - He listened.
    - He asked questions.
    - He understood.
    - He gave answers.

12. We miss opportunities to communicate because everywhere we go, we talk.

13. As leaders, we need to:
    - Try to empathetically understand the other person's position.
    - Realistically determine whether we are dealing with a won't or a can't.
    - Don't attach spiritual issues to a lack of response.
    - Make sure we broadcast on the other person's frequency (abstract or concrete).
    - Remember it is my responsibility to communicate effectively.

14. The most important conversations are the ones we have with ourselves.

15. Listening will ultimately help us to give better answers.

Note

1 "From the Editors," Leader to Leader, Summer 2002, www.pfdf.org/leader-books/l2l/summer2002/editors.html.

CHAPTER FOUR

DECISION MAKING

When you're 100% certain, you're too late.

—Charles W. Robinson

Maria's Maids is a successful cleaning business, and Maria would be happy if it weren't for one of her employees. Her newest hire, Lorna, is incompetent. Lorna was hired to clean, but she doesn't want to work alongside her coworkers. She was hired as a favor to a friend; but she always has a bad attitude, and she rarely shows up for work on time. However, Lorna's father manages three large businesses; and they all use Maria's cleaning services. Her father has also recommended Maria's Maids to other local businesses. Since he represents a significant source of revenue for Maria, firing Lorna could be bad for business. In addition, Maria's daughter and Lorna are friends. They hang out with the same group of people socially. Firing Lorna could affect her daughter. What should she do?

Situational and Principled **Leaders**

Either we are situational decision-makers or principled deci-sion-makers. We communicate who we are by the decisions we make. If Maria is a situational decision maker, she will be

> **Decision making is predictable when done by a principled leader.**

more concerned about her relationship with Lorna, Lorna's father, and her own daughter than she will about how Lorna's incompetence affects her business. As a situational leader, Maria would rather put up with Lorna's bad behavior than make a big deal out of it or risk causing conflict.

If Maria is a principled decision-maker, she will make the decision based on what she believes is right or wrong. She will realize it isn't fair to the other employees or to her customers to pay Lorna if she is incapable of doing the job. It is likely that Lorna will be fired, regardless of the personal consequences to Maria. While she obviously doesn't want to hurt her business or her daughter's friendship, she will make her choice based on what is right, not what is easiest.

As a principled leader, Maria will follow a detailed plan before firing Lorna. She will document everything that is going on, not only what she feels like recording. She will give Lorna additional training. She will have conversations and will involve other people if necessary. If Lorna's behavior still isn't resolved, she will not worry about the short-term consequences. If circum-stances call for it, she will terminate Lorna.

Decision making is predictable when done by a principled leader.

Employees of a principled leader feel secure because they know it is not who you know but how you act. Decisions are con-sistent, and they consider long-term consequences.

Situational leaders rarely think about future consequences.

(I need to concentrate on)

(They are mostly interested in avoiding conflict right now) Their decisions are inconsistent. People who work for situational leaders are rarely sure how the decision will be made. Employees may try to control the information the leader receives in an effort to influence her decision in a direction that is favorable to them. Working for a situational leader can be very difficult because the employee is always trying to second-guess what the leader's response will be, for it is rarely the same twice.

As I write this chapter, the media is reporting about a national company whose computers were hacked. This action resulted in the theft of confidential information affecting thousands of people. When confronted with the information, company officials denied the size of the problem but later had to admit it was larger than

> **Our decisions tell other people who we are.**

they thought. As the true size of the information breech became apparent, the company offered to make some changes. When those didn't appease government officials, it added a few minor concessions to their customers in an effort to avoid lawsuits. As the situation calls for it, they agree to do a little more.

This is an example of situational leadership. Officials are doing what they have to do to appease the situation without making drastic changes.

Instead, compare this one with the Tylenol® pain reliever incident over twenty years ago. When a couple of bottles of Tylenol® were tainted with cyanide, executives didn't say, "Well it's only in this small area." Instead, they removed every Tylenol® product off store shelves regardless of where the product was made, how it was wrapped, or where it was sold. These executives were principle driven.

It is important for us to understand how we make decisions because our decisions tell other people who we are.

Decision Making **Model**

Decision making is an art and a science. Sadly, most of us were never taught how to make good decisions, so we make decisions based on the situation. But we can learn to make better decisions if we analyze the steps we use.

Each time we make a decision, we follow several steps. Most of these happen unconsciously. The most common steps include gathering data, sorting out the information that is relevant to the decision, combining it with our knowledge, and then ultimately making a decision. Here's a closer look at these steps:

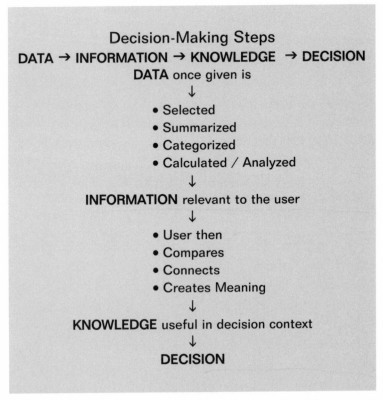

Decision-Making Steps
DATA → INFORMATION → KNOWLEDGE → DECISION
DATA once given is
↓
- Selected
- Summarized
- Categorized
- Calculated / Analyzed
↓
INFORMATION relevant to the user
↓
- User then
- Compares
- Connects
- Creates Meaning
↓
KNOWLEDGE useful in decision context
↓
DECISION

Let's say that Pat lives in North Georgia and needs to travel to South Atlanta for Grandma's birthday party. Doesn't seem like much of a decision, does it? Pat loves her cooking and nothing is better than spending Sunday dinner at Grandma's house since she always makes a feast. But to get to her house while the mashed potatoes are still hot, Pat has to make many decisions. Here's a demonstration of one: How will he get to Grandmother's house?

First Step: Data Collection. During this step, we collect all of the data that we need or could possibly need. For Pat, that data might include the answers to these questions:

- What time does dinner start?
- How early does he need to get there to get a seat at the adult table?
- What time does the Sunday worship service start and end at his church?
- Does he need to go home first, or can he leave directly after church?
- Will he be attending Sunday School that day?
- What subject will the pastor preach on?
- How long does it take to get to Grandma's?
- Will he be hungry when he gets there?
- Will he take I-75 or Highway 400?
- Which is the fastest route? Safest route?

Once Pat has gathered all the pieces of data, he begins selecting which ones are important, summarizing and categorizing them. Finally, he analyzes them and makes calculations based on the data.

Second Step: Select Relevant Information. At this point, Pat has to select which pieces of data are relevant to his decision. Whether or not he will be hungry and the topic of the pastor's sermon on Sunday won't affect his travel plans, so he can safely eliminate those pieces. By comparing and connecting the other bits of data, he can get information that is actually useful. Here are some pieces that will be meaningful for the decision he is about to make:

- He plans to attend the worship service at his church. It ends at 11:00.
- Grandma wants him at her place by 1:00.
- There are several ways to get there. If he takes Interstate 75, it will take approximately an hour and a half.
- Currently there is construction on I-75, and the traffic could delay him up to 45 minutes.

If he takes State Highway 400, it will take an hour and forty-five minutes, but there isn't any construction.

Step Three: Combine with Preexisting Knowledge. Now that Pat has the relevant information he can combine it with preexisting knowledge, such as the fact that if he is late for dinner not only will Grandma be mad, but Cousin Arthur will finish off the banana cream pie.

Step Four: Make Decision. At this point, Pat decides he will take Highway 400 because, while it may not get him there earlier, it will ensure that he is at Grandma's house on time. And the consequences of being late (and missing Grandma's banana cream pie) are too great. Decision made.

We follow these same steps each time we make a decision; but with most decisions, we do it so fast that we aren't conscious of it. This model tries to diagram that unconscious process, whether our choices involve driving directions, leadership, or even dating decisions. Regardless of the content, these same four steps are involved.

Understanding how we make decisions can help us get better at solving problems because we can test our assumptions at each step in the process. For example, if the data that we used to make a decision was wrong, the decision won't be a good one. If we incorrectly categorized or selected information that wasn't relevant, that step will influence our decisions. If our preexisting knowledge is wrong, then combining it with excellent data will still lead to a poor choice.

The ability to articulate each of the steps in our thinking process can help us to make better decisions. It can also lead to better relationships with the people we work with.

Decision Making Is an **Opportunity to Communicate**

When those around us make bad decisions, don't just come down hard on them; use this time as an opportunity to talk with them. Ask them how they made this decision. What process did they go through? Using the decision making model from above, ask them what data they started with. How did they decide which pieces of information were relevant to their decision? What existing knowledge did they combine with the data to make their decision?

> ### Ask These Questions in This Order
>
> 1. Is this decision in line with our vision, mission, and core values?
> 2. Do we have the organizational and human capacity to do this? Do we have the heart for this?
> 3. How will God be glorified?
> 4. How much will it cost?

Asking these kinds of questions will help us understand more about how they approach their own decision-making. More importantly, it will become an opportunity for us to teach them on how we would like them to make decisions in the future.

We can also explain why we did what we did, using this as an opportunity to refocus them on the vision, teach them better decision-making skills, and learn how their decision-making patterns differ from our own. In any organization, the better we understand our own decision-making blind spots and the blind spots of those who work with us, the better we can conquer them.

Four Questions to **Ask before Acting**

When presented with a complicated decision that could change the organization, we need to ask four questions; and it is important that we ask them *in this order*.

1. Is it in line with our vision, mission, and core values? No matter how great an idea or opportunity, if it isn't in line with the vision, we must say no to it.

2. Do we have the organizational and human capacity to do this? Do we have the heart for this? Maybe the program is so large that it would tax the entire team. Maybe we don't have the right people on the team to make this happen. Or maybe we don't want to do it at this time.

3. How will God be glorified? Most leaders will ask, "Will God be glorified?" and the answer is usually yes. Instead, ask, "How?" Answering this question will help us to understand the true impact this decision will have on God's Kingdom. Those in the secular marketplace can ask the same question with a slight twist: "How will this decision serve the community or my organization?"

4. How much will it cost? Understand this question, and then consider it carefully. It is not, "Can we afford it?" Most organizations don't have money sitting around waiting to be used. The answer is usually no. But the answer to "How much will it cost?" is different. The cost includes not only dollars, but people, resources, and the time and energy pulled from other projects and programs.

A program that won't make it past the question "Can we afford it?" might get a different response after asking these four questions. If the vision is big enough, if the people have a heart for doing it, if God will be glorified in a mighty way, then the money will come.

Answering these specific questions, *in this order,* helps us understand the true opportunity before us. We will be making a principled decision based on a larger organizational context, not on a situation, such as the amount of cash in the checkbook.

Practical Decision **Making**

The information above gives us a foundation for making good decisions, but there are a few practical tips that will help us as well.

Be able to explain why. We need to be able to articulate why we made the decision we did. This isn't so we can defend ourselves when

> **Junk short-term strategies that prevent long-term successes.**

we make a bad decision; it is so we can learn from all of our decisions. If we don't know why we did it in the first place, we will never get better at making decisions. Understanding how we make decisions will help us to make even better decisions in the future.

Be brave. Sometimes when we make decisions, we want to stay in our comfort zone and not go outside of it for additional data. This is a bad idea. Whenever possible we should seek information from those people or places that have it, even if it makes us uncomfortable. For example, ask:

"Who on my team will show me the things I most need to see?"

"Who will tell me things that are hard to hear?"

"Who is the best source for the information needed to make this decision?"

Be decisive. We won't always have all the information we need to make a decision. Sometimes the best thing we can do is make a decision without having all of the information. How do we know which decisions should wait and which we should move on? Put time into the decisions with the biggest payoff. Allow others to make those to which we can add little, even if we like making them.

imp   imp -
49   example Agape Place

Be willing to smash icons. We can't let turf wars, misuse of power, or phony motivation schemes affect our judgment. Resist the idea that loyalty is a one-way street. Junk short-term strategies that prevent long-term successes.

We make many decisions each day. Some of them are important, some of them are not. But the more we can pay attention to the process we use in making decisions, the better decisions we will make. For example, if Maria can separate her feelings for her daughter and her concerns about Lorna's father from her ability to take an unbiased look at Lorna's performance, she will make a good decision. If she can't, her other employees will know this is not someone they want to work for; and her customers won't be getting the service they expect.

Before we move to the next chapter, it is important to understand good decision-making because the number of decisions we will make increases exponentially with every person we hire. And like Maria, the most critical decision we make is deciding who is on our team.

Teaching Points

1. Situational leaders make decisions based on the current conditions without regard to future consequences.
2. Principled leaders make decisions based on what's right and wrong and pay attention to future consequences.
3. Decisions are made through a series of steps, whether or not we are conscious of the process.
4. Steps in the decision-making process:
   - Step 1: Collect data, any information that might be important.
   - Step 2: Select relevant information, and analyze and organize it.
   - Step 3: Combine relevant information with preexisting knowledge.

- Step 4: Finally, make the decision.
5. Decision-making is an opportunity to communicate what is important.
6. Ask these four questions in this order before making a big decision:
   - Is this decision aligned with our vision, mission, and core values?
   - Do we have the organizational and human capacity for this? / Do we have the heart for this?
   - How will God be glorified?
   - How much will it cost?
7. When making decisions:
   - Be able to articulate why we made the decision.
   - Be brave. Look outside of our comfort zone for information and answers.
   - Be decisive. Sometimes we have to make a decision regardless of whether we feel like we have enough information.
   - Be willing to smash icons.

CHAPTER FIVE

CHOOSING THE TEAM

> *It requires a lot of time and effort to make sure you have the right people working in the right jobs, but we believe this is time well spent. Customer satisfaction is the payoff.*

—Truett Cathy, founder of Chick-fil-A

Jim Collins and his team of twenty researchers spent five years and more than 15,000 man hours researching how some companies move from being merely good to being great. He included the findings in his book *Good to Great: Why Some Companies Make the Leap...and Others Don't.*

> **Start with the right people on the bus, and then decide where to go.**

One of his key findings was the importance of choosing the right employees. Here's a quote from his Web site:

> *The main point of this concept is not just about assembling the right team—that's nothing new. The main point is to first get the right people on the bus (and the wrong people off the bus) before you figure out where to drive it.*[1]

Collins makes the point that some people want to get on the

bus because of where it is going, but he suggests a better way. *Start* with the right people on the bus, and *then* decide where to go.

Proper People Placement **Prevents Problems**

The church hired Harry to head up the new focus on international missions. The church had decided to place an emphasis on global outreach and had many exciting plans to send teams to the outermost parts of the world. As the new leader of this team, Harry would be in a high profile position, requiring lots of travel where he would meet with other dignitaries on behalf of the church. Harry had traveled widely and liked attending meetings with other important representatives. He was excited about where the church was going and about his key leadership role in their plans.

But what happens if things change? What if the economy slows down, and the international focus has to be shifted to local outreach because of the increased costs of air travel and new airline security concerns? Instead of Harry doing international travel, the church decides to focus on local neighborhoods. No longer is Harry hanging out with important politicians; now he is witnessing to local street gangs and counseling elderly neighbors on their financial concerns. Unfortunately, all Harry wanted was a high profile position. He wanted to go where he thought the bus was going. Now the wrong person is on the bus, and the church has to figure out how to get him off.

Obviously, evangelism is important to the church. But what if instead of high profile Harry, the church had hired terrific Terry, the best evangelist they could afford? Terry could then decide where the bus should go. Knowing that the economy is tight, Terry believes he can find local opportunities to minister without incurring the costs of international travel. Terry would be happy talking to seniors and wayward teens, and if the economy picks up, he'll travel to witness internationally. Terry is happy talking to anybody because that's what he does best. Since he is called to be an evangelist, he doesn't care where the bus takes him to do that; he only cares whether or not his ministry is effective.

Harry was hired for *what* he knows, but Terry was hired for *who* he is. It's a different hiring philosophy. Hiring the best people and letting them help decide the direction of the bus will always be better than hiring people who want to go where they think the bus is going. If the bus breaks down or changes course, the latter group wants off.

In addition, some people are more comfortable in the front; others are back-of-the-bus servants. A newly hired leader might be a good candidate for the children's ministry; but if her true calling is drama, she'll be a better fit for the drama ministry. She is also likely to stay longer in a job that she is passionate about. Once the right people are on the bus, they need to have the right seats. In other words, proper people placement prevents problems!

No **Volunteers!**

When it comes to putting people on the bus, don't ask for volunteers. My experience as both a pastor and a business leader is that people who volunteer usually aren't the most qualified. Whether the position is paid or unpaid, those who volunteer are likely to be less experienced than the team members we recruit. The wrong people are often the ones to volunteer first. How does a volunteer get unvolunteered if the situation doesn't work out? The most qualified people are busy and engaged elsewhere. They won't come along unless someone recruits them.

The best stereotyped Sunday school teacher may not be the

one who offers to do it. The person for the job might be the public school teacher who doesn't think she wants to spend another day with kids. However, if a leader takes time to share the vision for Sunday school and she can see there is support from the top down, it's possible to change her mind.

With my busy travel schedule, I rarely volunteer to do things; but when someone recruits me for a position, I am much more inclined to do the job. When Jesus needed disciples, he didn't look around to see who would volunteer. Instead, he went out and chose the men he wanted:

> *Ye have not chosen me, but I have chosen you, and ordained you, that ye should go and bring forth fruit, and that your fruit should remain: that whatsoever ye shall ask of the Father in my name, he may give it you"(John 15:16, KJV).*

He chose them and ordained them, so they would go and bring forth fruit. That should be our goal when hiring people. When seeking the proper person to fill a job, the résumé can't help you make this kind of decision; the Holy Spirit must draw us to the right candidate, sometimes even in spite of the résumé.

Recruiting **Tips**

Remember the dodge ball games so many of us played in physical education classes? The teacher would pick two kids to be captains of the teams. The captains would take turns picking who they wanted to be on their teams. First, they chose the best athletes; then they chose their friends. As they neared the end of the pickings, they tried to choose the best of the least until only one kid was

> ASK candidates are recruited because of their attitude, skills, and knowledge, the three things needed for players on a winning team.

left. The last kid picked always felt like a loser.

Now that we're the leaders, we face similar choices. How do we assemble a winning team? Should we pick our friends out of loyalty? Should we choose the people who are best qualified? Some have even chosen the least qualified because they mistakenly believe it is about ministering to job applicants. But to truly serve others, we have to have quality people.

When choosing people for the team, remember the acrostic ASK. Unlike people who volunteer, ASK candidates are recruited because of their *attitude, skills,* and *knowledge,* the three things needed for players on a winning team.

Attitude. When we hire people with the right attitude, we can teach them to do anything. A good attitude can help a person conquer the most difficult circumstances. Employees with good attitudes work hard, are driven to reach goals, and continue to press on regardless of the roadblocks. People with bad attitudes are unmotivated, negative, and self-absorbed. No matter how talented they are, they never amount to much.

William James, a 19th-century psychologist and philosopher, said, "The greatest discovery of any generation is that a human being can alter his life by altering his attitude." People with good attitudes are teachable, correctable, and redirectable. Sales managers often say they want to hire someone who is "hungry." They aren't talking about someone who needs to eat; they're talking about someone who wants to

> **"We hire people for what they know and fire them for who they are."**

get out there and sell, someone who is motivated. They're describing an attitude.

Skill. If the church needs a piano player, the church needs someone with the skills to read music, keep time, and work with other musicians. But there must be a balance between attitude and skill.

Ginger Rae and Donna Lowe, human resource consultants, said, "We hire people for what they know and fire them for who they are." Their skills are the *what*. Their attitude is the *who*. An eager teenager who can't play but has a positive outlook won't cut it on Sunday mornings. Likewise, who wants to worship to the sound of music made by a virtuoso player with a cranky attitude? Finding a balance is important.

Knowledge. The person who has a great attitude, superb skills, and also extensive knowledge is the ideal employee or team member. Those with skill and knowledge can fix what is broken and explain why it broke in

> **People are most productive when they are passionate about what they are doing.**

the first place. But knowledge without skill is like a doctor who can make a diagnosis but doesn't know how to treat the illness.

Candidates with the right balance of ASK need to be asked what they want to do. If they are forced into jobs that don't suit their temperaments and passions, they won't be fully productive. People are most productive when they are passionate about what they are doing. Always try to put people into positions they care about. Of course, the only way to do so is to know them and understand their passions.

Know Your Team

After a team is recruited, spend time learning about them as individuals. Specifically, look at these four A's:

Attitudes. This is who they are. Discover who they are by understanding their attitudes toward their jobs and the people around them.

Affinities. What do they like? Who do they like? Some team members may have an affinity for a previous leader. Knowing those alliances are still there can help current leaders to make a smooth transition.

Anxieties. What causes them stress? Who causes them stress? If a particular executive creates stress among employees, running interference can enable them to concentrate on their jobs. If a monthly report keeps them up at night, changing it to a quarterly report could make them more efficient.

Animosities. What is it and who is it they don't like? Maybe a predecessor eliminated hour-long lunches in favor of leaving early; but if employees hate the new policy because

> **The A's of a Team**
> **Attitudes**
> **Affinities**
> **Anxieties**
> **Animosities**

the lunch hour is when they typically ran personal errands, a simple change could make them happier. Understanding their animosity allows us to make changes.

Leaders can only react to information if first they know about it. So take time to get to know your players.

Team Members **Know**

Team members know who is performing and who isn't performing. If asked, they will provide assessments about which people are doing their jobs and those who are doing them exceptionally well. Often an underperforming worker on a team causes unhealthy conflict. Understanding the situation from the perspective of other team members allows us to make informed decisions.

Team members also know who the toxic people are. They can name the person with the bad attitude, the one who is irritable all the time, and the one person who makes their lives miserable. Replacing these people with encouraging and inspiring team members can help the entire organization function better. In fact, they may help the team rise to a level they previously couldn't reach.

Consider the fact that while John the Baptist was still in Elizabeth's womb, he didn't leap in the presence of ordinary people. It wasn't until Mary came to visit with the miracle baby inside of her, that John leaped inside of Elizabeth's womb. The moral of the story? People pregnant with good things can cause your team to leap and soar.

> **Team members know who is performing and who isn't performing.**

Consider this quote from Charlie Crystle, founder of Chili!Soft:

> *The number one thing you need to understand about building a company is that mediocre people drag down excellent people—they are cancer and you need to cut them out as fast as possible. Don't worry about creating holes in the company—excellent people are much more productive when mediocre people are removed from their environment.*[2]

It isn't that we don't have enough people on the team, according to Crystle; it's that we have the wrong people on the team. If we ask our people, they will tell us who the problem is.

Annual **Review**

We can learn important insight from our employees all year long, but perhaps the best time is during their annual reviews. They can take this opportunity to give us feedback on how things are working, and we can take time to discuss their concerns. This is also the time we must decide whether to retain, retrain to reassign, or release a particular team member.

> **People pregnant with good things can cause your team to leap and soar.**

Always hire slowly, but fire quickly. Leaders often regret that they had not fired people the first time they thought about it, rather than letting a situation continue. I've never met anyone who said, "Gee, I wish I had let him stay a little longer." Usually it is the opposite. "Wow, I am glad she's gone. Wish I had done that sooner." Why do we tolerate bad employees? **Hire slowly, fire quickly.** The first time you seriously consider firing someone is the best time to do it.

Finally, the annual assessment is a chance for us to look over our team as a whole. Do we have the team we need to get the job done? Do we have the leaders we need to support us? The leaders who got us here may not be the leaders we need to take advantage of upcoming opportunities. That's why leadership selection is critical to the future.

Selecting Your **Leaders**

The most critical decision we make is selecting the leaders who will be on our team. When looking for leaders, there are two characteristics found in people who work for us. They either think and act like managers or they think and act like leaders.

Leaders think about the future and then work back to the present as they decide what to do. They might say, "In the future we will need to do that, so we'd better begin with this today." They focus on the big picture. They like innovative thinking and are often full of big ideas. They are excited by change and move quickly once they have identified new opportunities. Leaders are willing to take risks. They are people and idea centered; and while they hope people like what they do, they don't have to have personal approval to do their jobs.

Contrast this with a managerial attitude. Managers conceptualize plans by working from the past to the present. They might say things like, "This is how we've always done it." They have a microperspective of situations and examine them as snapshots. They favor routine thinking and are protectors of the status quo. Unlike leaders, they emphasize *how* and *when* rather than *what* and *why*. Managers are controlling and directing, and they are threatened by change. When it occurs, they move slowly, identifying obstacles in their way. They avoid risks, and their actions are limited to the available resources. They are plan and system centered, and they very much need the approval of those they work with and for.

Leaders:	Managers:
• Emphasize what and why.	• Emphasize how and when.
• Work from the future back to the present.	• Work from the past to the present.
• Focus on the long term.	• Focus on the short-term or immediate issues.
• Embrace a macroperspective.	• Embrace microperspectives.
• Favor innovative thinking.	• Favor routine/safe thinking.
• Seek to balance idealism with realism.	• Emphasize pragmatism over idealism.
• Show revolutionary flair.	• Protect the status quo.
• Clarify the vision, inspire and motivate.	• Implement the vision.
• Are excited by change.	• Are threatened by change.
• Decide quickly.	• Decide slowly.
• Identify opportunities.	• Identify obstacles.
• Take risks.	• Avoid risks.
• Pursue resources.	• Limit actions to available resources.
• Are people centered.	• Are system centered.
• Are idea centered.	• Are plan centered.
• Focus on core issues.	• Are distracted by peripheral issues.
• Want others' approval.	• Need others' approval.
• Do the right thing.	• Do things right.

When I refer to manager, I am not saying the word as a job title. People who have the job title of manager can act like leaders or managers. The biggest difference is that managers get the most out of themselves; leaders get the most out of others. That's why good leaders are so critical. They will permeate every level of an organization. Whenever possible we should hire people with leadership characteristics.

In the introduction, I mentioned my book, *Who's Holding Your Ladder?: Selecting Your Leaders—Leadership's Most Critical Decision*. In it, I discussed the five key qualities needed. Leaders (or ladder holders) must be:

- *Strong:* They can handle instruction and correction.
- *Attentive:* They pay attention and learn quickly.
- *Faithful:* They believe in their leaders.
- *Firm:* Manipulative people cannot blow them about.
- *Loyal:* They don't question their leader's motivations just because they don't like his method.

These qualities are important because the leaders selected will be holding the ladder. If they aren't quality people who are good at what they do, the ladder will be shaking in the wind. We will never be able to climb to the top. But if they are superior ladder holders, we won't fear climbing to the top and standing on the highest rung because we know they will keep the ladder from shaking.

Superior leaders don't have to be reminded constantly. They are intentional in their approach to their work. They are faithful to the vision of the organization, and they are not looking around to see if there is anything better out there. They are building our organization, rather than building their résumé.

But to get that kind of reliable performance, leaders must get training. Few people have ladder holders who are qualified and trained. In most organizations, we have a lot of followers and a few leaders. That is why it is important to mentor and develop the potential in future leaders. Following Jim Collins's advice will ensure the best people are on the bus and that the bus is pointed in the right direction. Ultimately, we must be the drivers who control who gets on and off and where they sit.

Teaching Points

1. Proper people placement prevents problems.
2. Do not ask for volunteers regardless of whether it is a paid or unpaid job. Instead, recruit people with the needed qualifications.
3. When hiring people remember they must have a balance of ASK:
   - Attitude: People with good attitudes are teachable.
   - Skill: The ability needed to do the job.
   - Knowledge: Personal experience and insight they can bring with them.
4. A leader must know who is on the team. Be informed about who they are by understanding their:
   - Attitudes
   - Affinities
   - Anxieties
   - Animosities
5. Team members know who is performing and who isn't.
6. Decide during the annual review whether a team member should be retained, reassigned and retrained, or released.
7. Leaders are the foundation of an organization. Select ladder holders who are:
   - Strong
   - Attentive
   - Faithful
   - Firm
   - Loyal

Notes

1 www.jimcollins.com/lab/firstWho/index.html

2 "You Must Hire the Right People," BusinessWeek Online, March 26, 2003, www.businessweek.com/smallbiz/content/mar2003/sb20030326_3034.htm.

CHAPTER SIX

LEADERSHIP DEVELOPMENT

Do the vice presidents at Ford Motor Company think of themselves as "car guys"? Do the leaders at Unilever think of themselves as "soap makers"? Do the executives at Wal-Mart think of themselves as "retail specialists"?

—Jennifer Schuchmann, author of Your Unforgettable Life

At children's birthday parties, there is often an abundance of helium balloons, and without fail one of those balloons will escape from the clutches of a child and float away. The balloon rises to the highest point in the room and stops. For it to go higher, someone would have to raise the ceiling. To prove this, I can take the balloon outside and let it go. The same balloon now rises higher than the house, floats up into the sky, and eventually disappears from view.

In all organizations, there are balloons and ceilings. The balloons represent people who rise to a certain level and then stop. Leaders often function as ceilings, preventing the balloons from rising higher.

For example, a leader who fears risks discourages employees from taking them. A leader who is threatened by the talents of a high-performer won't give her high profile tasks because he fears she may succeed. These leaders are the ceiling that keeps the balloon from going higher. If we can increase the heights of their leadership ability, the balloons will rise too. Just like the balloon I released outside the house, there will be no stopping a talented employee from her ascent.

Leaders Can Raise **the Ceiling**

There are important implications in this illustration. The first is that instead of criticizing our employees saying, "Why isn't she doing that?" or "How come he never does that?" we need to consider the idea that we may be the ceiling stopping their upward progress. Looking at the situation from the perspective of the balloon can change our attitudes.

> We can raise our leadership ceiling and help everyone rise higher.

This doesn't mean that people around us never do anything wrong. A balloon can still have a leak; but if we take a broader look at our organization and stop blaming individuals, we can do something about it. We can raise our leadership ceiling and help everyone rise higher. That's what leadership development is all about. It's not only getting a single balloon to fly higher; it's learning to remove the roof to set all the balloons free.

Quality **Leaders**

Leaders are the people who hold our ladders while we climb toward our visions. They are also the people who keep the ladder steady when it is shaken by challenges. So how can we have the best leaders? Dr. Gerald Brooks, senior pastor of Grace Outreach Center in Plano, Texas says, "We have three choices."

The first is to do it ourselves. The advantage of this plan is that we are always in control. But we are also likely to face burnout. If we choose this option, people who work in this environment cease all upward movement. Employees who want to go higher than our leader-imposed ceilings will seek opportunities elsewhere. The organization will rise and fall with our strengths and weaknesses.

A second option is to hire the best leaders money can buy. Unfortunately, most organizations don't have unlimited budgets. There is a big gap between what we need and what we can afford.

The third option is to develop leaders internally. This is the least expensive option, but it is also the riskiest. What happens when trained leaders suddenly find better offers? The time spent (and it will take an incredible amount of time) will be wasted, right? But as Zig Ziglar said, "The only thing worse than training employees and losing them is not training them and keeping them."

While each of these options has advantages and disadvantages, the solution obviously has to be the third one. It's not that the disadvantages are less than the other two options; it's that the advantages to this option are far superior than the advantages of the others. Developing leaders isn't

> **Three Leadership Choices**
> 1. Do it yourself; too much work.
> 2. Hire it out; too much money.
> 3. Develop others; too much time.
>
> In the end, developing others yields the best rewards.

an endgame where leaders only become effective when they are fully actualized. Instead, time spent developing leaders returns itself in a roof that is raised across the organization. More importantly, mentoring others also helps us to grow.

Just as the leader determines the ceiling for his employees, we determine the ceiling for the leaders who work for us. This balloon and ceiling illustration holds true at every level. If I become a better father, my family can go higher. If I become a better Sunday school teacher, the class goes higher. If I become a better leader, the entire organization rises with me.

Leaders: **Born or Made?**

A recent television reality show featured three chefs in a competition. They received the same list of ingredients and were to prepare several courses. Each chef had the same amount of time and could use only the ingredients on the list. When the gourmet meals

> Mentoring others also helps us to grow.

were finished, a panel of judges picked the winner. This is a good example of what happens during leadership development. Given the same individual, different mentors develop leaders differently; and, of course, leaders respond to each mentoree differently.

There are several implications here. Leaders should have multiple people developing them. Not only should we develop the leaders under us, but we should encourage them to seek outside mentors who can also develop their ingredients.

People often say, "He is a born leader." I respectfully disagree. Leaders aren't born; they're made, like bread is made. Leadership development is an intentional activity. Raisin bread doesn't appear by itself even if we leave the ingredients on the kitchen counter overnight. Someone must consciously take ingredients and knead them together, put the mixture under the right amount of heat and allow it to rise, then punch it down and start over again until the dough is the perfect consistency. Only then will it rise above the pan. Helping a leader rise takes this same kind of intentional activity.

I believe everyone has the ingredients needed to be a leader. We are leaders at different times and places. Dad might be a manager in an office. The people who work for him acknowledge that he is a leader. But Mom is also a leader. She leads a Cub

Scout troop, she leads the family in getting chores done, and every morning she leads the kids to school. But Junior could be a leader too. Maybe he is the academic pacesetter of the fourth grade or is the captain of the dodgeball team at recess. Even the dog can lead with his bark when a stranger comes to the front door. So if everyone is capable of being a leader, how do we explain the difference in ability between leaders?

If we could measure people on a leadership scale of one to ten, some people will only rise to a level three while others will rise to a ten.

> **If I become a better leader, the entire organization rises with me**

The ingredients are there, but they never seem to come together to their full potential. That's where we come in. With the proper training, dogs are taught to lead blind people through busy streets. What can our leaders accomplish if we invest time in developing them?

Key Leadership **Ingredients**

There are three key ingredients that when properly combined affect leadership development. The first is the raw material itself. An individual's intelligence, physical and emotional health, energy level, and personality will all play a part in the kind of leader they become.

The second is the context in which they are developed. Some leaders develop better through quiet, one-on-one coaching. Other leaders learn through trial and error, working through demanding leadership challenges while being encouraged from the sidelines.

The third ingredient is the person doing the development. Ultimately, a mentor can only teach what she already knows.

Just like the cooking show, the result of leadership development is determined by how the mentor uses the ingredients in a given context. A shy leader may need quiet supportive coaching. If he is trained by a mentor who believes in trial-by-fire, the leader won't grow much. Likewise, if the developing leader thrives on challenges but doesn't have hands-on opportunities to practice his new skills, he will not reach his full potential.

Developing and mentoring leaders is like teaching babies to walk. First, the parents help them stand on their own without falling down. Once the baby has mastered standing, the parents move a few feet away and encourage baby to take a step. Eventually the parents move across the room and entice them to come. If babies get started in the wrong directions, parents turn them around. When it appears the babies might run into obstacles, parents rush to protect them. And, of course, a good parent always picks the baby up when she falls and helps her start over again.

> There is no such thing as a fully developed leader. It's a myth.

It takes time for babies to learn to walk, and it takes time for leaders to develop their skills. It is a learning process that continues. There is no such thing as a fully developed leader. It's a myth.

In my book *Who's Holding Your Ladder?: Selecting Your Leaders—Leadership's Most Critical Decision* I talk about being an accidental leader. Until recently, I was never mentored, so mentoring others didn't come easy to me. As a result, the mentoring I did was also accidental. I thought mentoring others meant recommending good management books I had read. I didn't intentionally create leaders; consequently, when I saw leaders rise on their own, I didn't know what to do with them. In some cases, I felt threatened by their potential, so I did stupid things to lower the ceiling. As a result, we all became dysfunctional.

I've matured through those experiences and now know that I had to grow personally before I could successfully mentor others. One of the keys to my own growth was surrounding myself with people who are better than I am. Sometimes new leaders find doing so intimidating; they're afraid their candles don't shine as brightly in a room full of bonfires. They prefer to stay in the dark where they have the only light shining. But the truth is that we don't know it all and we shouldn't be afraid to ask for help. Understanding our own inadequacies means we're less likely to pass them on. Learning from those who are more experienced and being humbled by our own limitations can help us develop and more fully develop others.

At this time, I have eleven mentors who each speak to me about a different area of my life. How did I find these mentors?

1. I categorized each area of my life that needed ongoing mentoring and coaching.

2. I identified people with specialized knowledge and skill in those areas.

3. I asked them.

Mentoring **How-To**

So what is mentoring? John C. Crosby, executive director of The Uncommon Individual Foundation, an organization devoted exclusively to mentoring, said, "Mentoring is a brain to pick, an ear to listen, and a push in the right direction." In his book *The Kindness of Strangers*, Marc Freedman wrote, "Mentoring is mostly about small victories and subtle changes." They're right. Mentoring isn't about the big things; it is about the small ones.

I believe that developing a leader begins by spending time with her. Does she know what her gifts are? Is she using them? If not, help her to develop both the understanding and practice of her unique gifts. Doing so can help us establish trust as she sees that we're not trying to change her, we're only trying to make her a better version of who she already is.

In my last book, *Who Moved Your Ladder?: Your Next Bold*

Move, I described in detail how I mentored Dr. Benson Karanja. He started at Beulah Heights Bible College as a janitor and now serves as the president of the college. Mentoring Benson involved introducing him to other executives and positioning him as someone of importance in their eyes. I believed in him and demonstrated this by taking risks with him. I enlarged his world by helping him to connect with people outside his comfort zone. Everyone stands under the same

> **Everyone stands under the same sky, but not all of us have the same horizons.**

sky, but not all of us have the same horizons. So I tried to push Benson's horizons back, so he could see more. This helped him perceive himself differently and self-perception has a lot to do with leadership development.

As Jennifer Schuchmann wrote, "Do the vice presidents at Ford Motor Company think of themselves as 'car guys?' Do the leaders at Unilever think of themselves as 'soap makers'? Do the executives at Wal-Mart think of themselves as 'retail specialists'?" No. When executives reach a certain level of leadership, it is no longer about managing the product or service. It is about leading people. If the executives at these companies depended on their ability to make cars, manufacture soap, and sell toiletries, they wouldn't be defined as great leaders. True leadership has to do with

> **Good leaders easily transition from company to company because their talents aren't in products they are in people.**

managing people and ideas. That's why good leaders can easily transition from company to company or even industry to industry. Their talents aren't demonstrated in their products; they're demonstrated in their people.

Sometimes we forget that developing leaders has little to do with training. We are not developing the skills. We are developing the leaders. I deliberately use the term *developing* rather than *training.* There is a vast difference between training people and developing them. Training focuses on tasks; developing focuses on the person. Training is unidirectional; developing is omnidirectional. We train people to become receptionists. When they are finished, they're good receptionists

> There is a vast difference between training people and developing them.

and they do their tasks well. We have not developed them, so they are ready to move into other positions.

That's why I believe we have a responsibility to *develop* leaders strategically and spiritually. When developing others, we need to spend as much time on the internal life, as we do on the parts we can see. Leadership is a matter of how to *be,* not how to *do.* This is the *who,* not the *what.*

When I was in college, I painted houses. But I was much more than a painter. I was a scraper; I had to remove old paint. I was a caulker, making sure the seams were sealed. I was a surface preparer; I did whatever it took to make sure the surface would absorb the paint. If I didn't do all of those other jobs first, my paint job would not have been pleasing to the homeowner.

In the same way, we need to prepare the leaders we develop. They have to be cultivated at a personal level. We need to help them scrape off the peeling paint, seal the seams, and prepare the surface for what we're about to do with them. If we don't take the time to make sure the individual is ready, our mentoring will be for naught. The person will be like a stain on the wall that wasn't treated with primer. It remains

> Leadership is a matter of how to be, not how to do.

unchanged regardless of how many times we paint over it. But if we take the time to properly prepare people, then our mentoring will help them change from the inside out.

Leaders must understand that to truly develop, they must

first work on themselves; only then can they focus on others. Working on self includes all the touchy-feely things on the inside of who they are. It also includes basic things about their jobs, such as getting the work done, holding their people accountable for what they do, and staying focused. Once they've gotten a handle on self, they can move to focusing on others. Working toward gaining commitment from their team, managing conflict, and overcoming obstacles.

Perhaps the best way to see progress in the people we are mentoring is when we notice they are mentoring other people. They've moved from leading projects to managing people. Not everyone we try to develop will make this transition. Some will try and fail and never try again. But when we see that leader finally take ownership over developing another leader, we might actually see the roof rise.

> **A Leader ...**
> Sees it (knows).
> Pursues it (grows).
> Helps others see it (shows).

What Happens When **I Am Not Here?**

Ignoring the need for a successor doesn't give me job stability. I should be developing people now who can step in and fill my job at any time. Some leaders find this process threatening. What if the people I train become more successful than me? What if they are better at doing my job than I am?

These fears are natural, but we have to set them aside. Eventually the ceiling will rise; we should be the one to do it. Having additional leaders at the top can help to raise high the roof beams. Think how much an organization could grow if there were two at the top. What if there were four or maybe even sixteen top leaders? Training leaders to do what we do doesn't have to be an exit strategy; it can be an expansion strategy.

An orchestra director who leads hundreds of professional musicians was asked, "What is the hardest instrument to play?" He didn't hesitate in his reply. "Second fiddle. Anybody can play first chair, but playing second chair is much more difficult."

This makes sense. Those in the second seat are often doing the same type and amount of work as those in the first chair. In some instances, they may be doing more if they run interference by keeping people away from the top position. They get less recognition and less compensation; and should a string break,

> Training leaders to do what we do doesn't have to be an exit strategy; it can be an expansion strategy.

they must be willing to pass their instruments over to the first chair players.

When the first chair leaves, the second chair must also overcome the stereotypes and rumors that she wasn't good enough to be there in the first place and still find a way to do her job. Helping those in the second chair be prepared shouldn't be threatening, it should be an honor.

When our terms end, we can leave behind three things. The first is memories. The second is a well-developed leader. The third, and perhaps most important, is a roof that is higher than when we came in.

Teaching Points

1. Balloons can only go as high as the ceiling. Leaders often act as a ceiling holding back their team.
2. Three leadership choices are:
   - Do it yourself; too much work.
   - Hire it out; too much money.
   - Develop others; too much time.

   In the end, developing others yields the best rewards.
3. Leaders aren't born; they're made through intentional development.
4. Everyone has leadership capability.
5. Three ingredients to leadership development are:
   - The raw material: an individual and his or her personal resources.
   - The context in which the person will be developed.
   - The person doing the development.
6. Developing leaders is like teaching a baby to walk. It must be done step-by-step.
7. Those who were accidental leaders become accidental mentors, teaching only what they know.
8. To grow, we must be surrounded by people who are better than we are.
9. We don't know it all.
10. We shouldn't be afraid to ask for help.
11. Developing leaders has little to do with training them. First they must develop themselves. Then they can focus on others.
12. Leadership is how to be, not how to do.
13. Measure progress by leaders who learn to lead and then use their gifts to develop others.
14. Ignoring the need for a successor doesn't give us job stability.
15. When we're gone, make sure the roof is higher than when we came in.

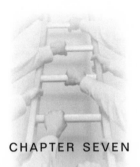

CHAPTER SEVEN

CHANGE VS. TRANSITION

*Life is pleasant. Death is peaceful. It's the transition
that's troublesome.*

—Isaac Asimov, novelist and scholar

Teisha had been in charge of the accounting department at
her company for over seven years and had been successful.
Recently her boss Matt, asked if she would consider moving to
the marketing department. He needed a seasoned manager to
handle things in that area. Always interested in numbers, the
new challenges of marketing analysis interested her. She agreed
to make the move. On Monday, Matt announced the change;
Teisha packed up her stuff and moved to an office on the seventh
floor near the marketing team. The change was easy, but the transition was not.

As soon as Matt announced Teisha's change, the gossiping
started. Was an accountant qualified to lead marketing? Who
would be the next accounting manager? Was Teisha responsible
for the previous marketing manager's firing? John had worked in
marketing for five years; why wasn't he picked to be the

marketing manager? Didn't Matt know people in the marketing department didn't like Teisha because she always demanded receipts for their reimbursements? And so it went.

Change vs. **Transition**

Change is the result of a decision. It is an external event. Moving Teisha from accounting to marketing is a change. It was announced, she moved her office, it is done.

Transition, on the other hand, is the emotional, relational, financial, and psychological processing of change. Transitions are internal. In this example, the transition included fears about the new leadership, affinities with the old marketing manager, animosities from existing marketing team members towards Teisha, misplaced alliances, and many other people problems Matt didn't identify or ignored before the change.

Understanding the difference between change and transition can help leaders plan appropriately. It is rare that change itself causes problems; typically, the culprit is a lack of transitional planning. Leaders are responsible for foreseeing and creating a strategy for transition in their organizations. But often, we spend so much time on change, we never strategically think through the transitional issues.

Transitional **Plans**

To be a good CEO or pastor, it isn't enough to only think through what we're going to do. We must also take time to write down all of the contingencies and create a written transitional plan.

Before the change Matt should have made a list of all the issues he could foresee. What vacuum would he create with this change? In this case, the accounting department would be without a manager.

What situation results from this change? It appears that Teisha could be in a situation where her team doesn't respect her. As a leader, what can Matt do to help her earn the respect she needs? Can he pass some of his credibility on to her? Credibility is a people problem, but it's not the only relational problem to consider during a transition. Other personnel issues that need thought include:

- Which people does the change affect?
- Of those people, who are the ones who care?
- Who cares deeply?
- Of those who care deeply, who will be positive about this change and who will not?

The main question is: How do I position Teisha for success?

After thinking through these questions, the leader must create a written plan and then make strategic decisions based on the plan. For example, consider:

- How will I approach each person?
- How will I communicate the details to him or her?
- What information will that person need to understand this change?

Here's another illustration. Tim is our worship leader. He gets caught in some kind of sin, and we have to discipline him. We ask him to step down from his position. But problems arise when some of the women think we weren't hard enough on him, the men think we were too hard on him, the young people think there was nothing wrong with what he did, and the old people wonder how many leaders are also doing what Tim did. Tim's mama is upset; and his daddy, who is on the church board, is mad at the leadership.

See what is happening?

Moving him out of his role as worship leader was the change. It was not a big deal to make that change. What will come back to bite us are the transitional issues. We need to map out all the contingencies, knowing that some of these plans will happen and others we won't have to worry about. We can't plan everything, but as much as possible we want to think through the transitional issues.

Matt needs to think systemically about the change he's made. He needs to remember that a change in one department will affect all the other departments. It is systemic thinking. Once the transition is worked through and people feel secure, the change is a nonissue. Leading change is easy if we first understand how to manage the transition.

How to **Transition**

William Bridges is a noted expert on change and transition. In his most recent book, *Managing Transitions: Making the Most of Change,* he explains that the reason change agents fail is because they focus on the solution instead of the problem. He believes that 90 percent of a leader's efforts should be spent on selling the problem and helping people understand what is *not* working. He rightly claims that people don't perceive the need for a solution if they don't have a problem.

> The reason change agents fail is because they focus on the solution instead of the problem.

Let's say I have an administrative assistant who is not working out. She comes in late, has a bad attitude, and is incompetent in her job. Firing her would solve that problem; but before I can fire her, I need to consider how this action would affect her coworkers. Currently she gets a lot of sympathy from them. They enable her behavior and encourage me to do the same by saying things like, "Don't you realize she's pregnant and recently had to change apartments?"

This is also where lawsuits can become transitional issues. Firing a pregnant woman without cause could bring legal trouble for me and the company. I must be sure the problem is understood. Of course, I am aware that she is failing to be a good assistant but I have to help others in the office understand that her inability to do her job is a problem for all of us. If I don't, they will be the first to undermine me by saying to the new assistant, "Did you know that he fired the pregnant woman who was here before you?"

So part of the transition must be helping people understand the problem, so they can more quickly agree on a solution.

In my book *Who Moved Your Ladder?: Your Next Bold Move,* I spent a lot of time talking about transitional issues. I used the example of my resignation from Beulah Heights Bible College. Instead of just resigning, I personally traveled all over the country to meet with board members and tell them what I was going to do and why. I even developed a possible successor.

In making that change, I had a transition plan. I knew who I was going to talk to, when I was going to talk to them, and what I was going to say. I can vouch from my personal experience that the time spent thinking and planning the transition made what could have been a negative occurrence a time of positive growth for me and the college.

Leaders Are Responsible **for Transitions**

A successful transition isn't the responsibility of the people undergoing the change. The responsibility for a successful transition belongs to the leader making the change. In one of my seminars, a young woman named Regina said she was moved from a small role in the children's department to a larger responsibility as Christian education minister. Regina did everything she could to prepare her people for a change. She found and trained her successor and helped transition her old team to their new leader.

But no one did the same for Regina. The pastor failed to make an announcement to the church that Regina was given this new responsibility. Further complicating matters, the former Christian education minister didn't realize that he was now out of a job and continued to function as if nothing had changed. This is a great example of a change without a transition. Regina had made the change; but without her pastor helping with the transition, she was now impotent in her new responsibility.

Some might wonder why a pastor would do that. I think I know. Regina is his daughter, and he was worried about how people would react to her taking on such an important role. He felt that she was the best person for the job, and she felt that she was ready. But without handling the transition properly, no one else at the church had that same confidence. Now he is trying to sort through the mess. He has both personal issues—after all, she's his daughter—and professional issues—his vision for this position in the church. In addition, when I first heard about the situation, Regina had been in her job for three months!

> **The responsibility for a successful transition belongs to the leader making the change.**

My recommendation to Regina was that her father go before the people and say, "My daughter, Regina, is going to provide great leadership to the Christian education ministry department at our church. Actually, she should have been functioning in this position for the last three months, but I have been remiss in not making that announcement. But I'm correcting that today. Come on up here, Regina, and tell them about your vision. What's God going to do with you?"

He will need to support her vision and have the people pray for her in her new role, sort of as a mini-inauguration. But he has to say something like, "I was remiss in not doing this before," so the people will know why he is doing this now and not then.

Assimilating new people into leadership roles is the hardest change issue we face. However, if we as leaders are aware of the differences between transitions and changes, if we properly prepare and execute a transitional plan, and if we take responsibility for the changes we bring on our people, the results will be worth the effort.

> Assimilating new people into leadership roles is the hardest change issue we face.

Teaching Points

1. Change is the result of a decision.
2. Transition is the emotional, relational, financial, and psychological processing of change.
3. Change is external. Transitions are internal.
4. Change can often be smooth. Transitions rarely are.
5. Leaders are responsible for foreseeing and creating a strategy for transition in their organizations.
6. A transitional plan must take into account all the contingencies, and it must be written down.
7. Leaders should consider the following two questions: What vacuum will be created with this change? What situation is created as a result of this change?
8. Other personnel issues that should be considered are:
   - Which people will be affected by the change?
   - Of those people, who are the ones who care?
   - Who cares deeply?
   - Of those who care deeply, who will be positive about this change? Who will be negative?
9. The transitional plan should include actions that need to be taken for each person involved and include instruction on:
   - How will I approach this person?
   - How will I communicate the details to him or her?
   - What information will this person need to understand this change?

10. William Bridges, the change expert, believes 90 percent of a leader's efforts should be spent on selling the problem. People don't need a solution if they don't have a problem.

11. A successful transition isn't the responsibility of the people undergoing the change. The responsibility for a successful transition belongs to the leader making the change.

12. Assimilating new people into leadership roles is the hardest change and transition issue we face.

CHAPTER EIGHT

CONFLICT

Everybody in America is soft, and hates conflict. The cure for this, both in politics and social life, is the same—hardihood.

—John Jay Chapman, author

The man had been shipwrecked and living on a deserted island for nearly four years when he heard the passing ship. He ran to the edge of the island, waving a torch to signal the boat. Fortunately, the captain saw him and ordered several crew members to go with him to investigate. As they neared the beachfront, they marveled at what they saw. The man had obviously done well with the meager supplies available to him.

"This is amazing," said the captain. "Before we go, do you mind giving my men and me a quick tour?"

"Not at all," said the relieved castaway. As he showed them around the small island, they noticed three huts.

"Why three huts?" asked the captain.

"I live in the first one," replied the man. "The second one is the church I go to. I thought it would be important to worship in a separate building."

The captain and his men were impressed. "So what is the third hut used for?"

"Oh, that is the church I *used* to go to."

The Purpose **of Conflict**

Church leaders often laugh when they hear this story. They immediately understand the humor because they also know people who have left churches for no apparent reasons. While people occasionally leave one church for another over honest theological differences, many more

> A lack of conflict doesn't signal progress, but it might signal inactivity.

leave because of unresolved conflict. To solve this problem, our goal shouldn't be to remove all conflict, but rather to help make our church members healthy. As leaders, it is important for us to understand conflict, its proper use, and how to best resolve it.

There is no such thing as a conflict-free zone. The only way to eliminate conflict is not to do anything. As long as there is movement or activity, engagement or involvement, there will always be conflict.

It's like the famous verse, "wherever there are two or three gathered, there's going to be conflict." Even in a marriage. Especially in a church. When a pastor tells me that he has a peaceful church and everybody gets along with everybody, I think, *Either you're out of touch or you're not doing anything.*

Sometimes we are so afraid of conflict that we walk toward peace and consensus when a little conflict might actually help the cause. A lack of conflict doesn't signal progress, but it might signal inactivity. Conflict is something that will always be. It is neither good nor bad, it simply is.

The Benefits **of Conflict**

Conflict serves a purpose. When there is conflict, we explore the issues surrounding that conflict more fully. The associated tension causes us to look deeper into a decision to make sure that we have all the information we need and we aren't overlooking anything. In essence, conflict becomes the motivation to make sure we examine the situation in detail. No one wants to be on the wrong side of an issue he didn't fully investigate.

When conflict is involved, people are often more committed to the final decision because they are confident that the issues have been examined from all sides and the best solution has been reached.

For conflict to be used positively it must involve dialogue with opposing parties *before* the decision is made. The actual process of making the decision becomes more important than the decision itself. Even people with contrary views will respond positively, or at least "agree to disagree," if they feel like their side was heard and understood by those making the decision.

The Dark Side **of Conflict**

But conflict can have a dark side as well. Consider a leader who faces unnecessary conflict over every decision she tries to make. It is like an electric fence used to keep a dog in the yard. The dog can't see it, but he knows not to cross the edge of the property line because he will get a mild shock. After attempting it several times, the dog soon learns it's better to avoid the borders altogether. When this happens to a leader, she is tempted to walk away from issues she needs to address because she fears the conflict. As a result, conflict can limit the scope of our leadership and make leaders reluctant to lead.

Likewise, personal conflict can affect our jobs. If I have a fight with my wife on the way to church on Sunday morning, by the time I get to the pulpit and begin to preach, she is all I can think about. I see her scowling at me from the front row, and I know she's thinking, *If only the people knew what I know. He should be the first one in line for the altar call!* It is hard to do a job well when distracted, and conflict in one area can leak into others. If we have conflict at work, it is hard not to bring that home to the family.

Each year, over 10,000 pastors in the United States resign because of irresolvable conflicts in their churches. The desire to avoid tough issues and distractions caused by conflict can skew our normally good judgment. Instead of facing conflict, we run from it. When we suppress our best instincts in an attempt to keep peace, we're not being true to our callings.

You Can't Please **Everybody**

We've all heard the old adage: "You can't please everybody." What I wish someone had told me was, "Sam, there will be blood on the floor. It may be yours, or it may be theirs, but to get where you're going, you may have to pay for it in blood." Of course, even if I had heard it, I probably wasn't in a place to understand it until I had been through it. But now I've learned; there is a price to be paid.

Discipline is just one example of necessary conflict. No one is going to send a thank-you card saying, "I know I was wrong, Pastor, and you love me so much you're setting me down for my own good. I know I'm going to grow through this experience. Thank you for loving me so much." No, instead there is going to be blood on the floor.

Like parents, leaders often have to discipline those who don't appreciate our actions. We try to do it in ways that prevent blood from spilling on the floor. We try to make it all neat and tidy.

However, a rocket ship can't get off the ground without a lot of heat and the sights, sounds, and fury that go along with it. Please understand, we can minimize the blood, but the blood will still be there.

Of course, I am not talking about literal blood on the floor; I am talking about the painful feelings aroused when we try to resolve conflict. I am also talking about the sacrifices made in the process. When my father disciplined me, he never drew real blood. But the shame of my actions often made me feel as if my blood had been spilled.

Some people like me; some people don't. We are all born with a need to be liked and approved; but sometimes in an effort to be accepted, we avoid conflict that is necessary. That's not good. While I am not suggesting that

> **The biggest factor in any conflict is the condition of the leader's health.**

we be conflict-lovers, we do need to find a way to come to terms with conflict. We need to be able to say, "I can't please everybody, and conflict is going to happen. It doesn't matter who I am or where I am at, sometimes there is just going to be blood on the floor."

Our Health Determines **Our Responses to Conflict**

If I cut my finger, it's going to scab over and heal. Depending on the size and location of the cut, it might leave a scar. But since I am healthy, it will eventually heal. If I were unhealthy, if I were a hemophiliac or had AIDS, the bleeding would be much harder to stop. I might get an infection or even bleed to death.

We need to view conflict in terms of our overall health. There is no such thing as a good marriage or a bad marriage, a good church or a bad church. There are only healthy marriages and unhealthy marriages, healthy churches and unhealthy churches.

The biggest factor in any conflict is the condition of the leader's health. We must be healthy when dealing with conflict.

We need to ask:

"Is this interaction healthy?"

"Is the way she's looking at me healthy?"

"The way I'm looking back, is that healthy?"

"What I'm just thinking, is that healthy?"

We shouldn't try to end in agreement or disagreement; we should try to end healthily. At the end of any difficult dialogue, we should always ask, "Are we still healthy?" because healthy relationships allow for transparency and open communication. The healthier the relationship, the more the transparency. But this transparency can be difficult because we each bring our own baggage into a relationship. That is why I must continually assess my own health. Before a difficult conversation, I ask, "How healthy am I?" because I can't help with their baggage until I've put mine away.

Different studies say different things, but approximately 50 percent of first-time marriages end in divorce; and the rate of divorce for second marriages is in the low 60s. This happens because someone in the marriage wasn't healthy. Instead of a better marriage the second time, an extra suitcase just got added to the baggage the couple was already carrying.

> **If we're healthy, we can help others get healthy too.**

We all have days when we are unhealthy, days where we feel like everything is bothering us. If I have important issues to deal with on a day that I am unhealthy, I postpone them. If something unhealthy is going on in my marriage and I have a counseling appointment with a young woman, I postpone the appointment. I call her and say, "Something has come up, and I need to reschedule." I don't have to say, "My wife this and her momma that." Likewise, if I have trouble with my finances, I won't go shopping on unhealthy days. If I have trouble keeping my tongue, I'll avoid situations in which I am likely to lose my temper.

We rearrange life on unhealthy days because we know that when we are healthy, people and things are not temptations. When we are unhealthy, however, that same person or activity can become intoxicating. When we are healthy, we can engage and disengage and shop or not shop. But when we're unhealthy, we have to make adjustments. An honest assessment of our own health and taking the appropriate actions on unhealthy days is the key to being able to handle conflict.

Remember Tim? He was the worship leader I disciplined in the last chapter. He left our church to go to Pastor Smith's church. Tim knows that Pastor Smith needs a worship leader. Tim attends for a few weeks. He has a few conversations with Pastor Smith, and guess what? Soon Tim is leading worship at Pastor Smith's church.

But the same thing that happened at our church is going to happen again at Pastor Smith's church. Why? Because Tim was hurt and disappointed by what happened. When he joined Smith's church, Pastor Smith didn't concentrate on getting him healthy. How do we know? If Tim were healthy, he would have come back to talk to his previous pastor. He would have said something like, "I am so sorry, and it will never happen again. I was totally out of line. Whatever discipline you want to impose on me would be welcomed." That would be creating health.

Many of us do what Pastor Smith did. We allow unhealthy people into our churches. Then instead of making them healthy, we give them new places to spread their dysfunctions. Tim left his last church under a spirit of conflict; he will bring that same spirit of conflict with him to his new church. We can't just hand him a microphone and tell him to lead worship. First we need to make sure he's healthy. If we're healthy, we can help others get healthy too.

So conflict should never be seen in the context of right or wrong, agreement or disagreement. Conflict should always be seen in the context of "Are we healthy?" Healthy people and healthy churches can go through conflict and heal from it.

Insecure People **Are Unhealthy**

Just because someone disagrees with me doesn't mean he is against me. My wife disagrees with me all the time. She isn't against me; she just disagrees. Bad health comes from insecurity. Consider 1 Corinthians 12:18: "But now hath God set the members every one of them in the body, as it hath pleased him" (KJV). What did God do in this verse? He *set* the members, every one of them, as it pleased him. This verse tells us that the setting is critical. Once we are secure in our setting, we can be healthy. When people are insecure and unhappy with where they are, then they get upset.

Brenda and I had been married for twenty-one years when she bought me a ring with a gold and silver setting that holds five diamonds. It also came with a not-so-romantic insurance policy. To keep the policy current, I have to take the ring every six months to the jeweler for an inspection. The jeweler looks at it and signs the warranty card. If a diamond should fall out, I can show him the warranty card to have it replaced at no cost.

When the jeweler checks the ring, he glances at the round part, barely looking at the gold and silver. He quickly counts the five diamonds. But in excruciating detail, he painstakingly examines the setting. If the setting is compromised, I could lose the diamonds. If the setting is intact, the ring will retain its value. So the setting is critical to the entire thing.

Think again about that verse. God has set every member as it pleased him. It is not about setting us where *we* want to be; he has set us in the setting where it pleases *him*. In Romans and

Ephesians, Paul talks about how we are all members or parts of the body. The place where the parts come together in a body is the joint. The joint is the setting. We need to have healthy joints in the setting where God has put us.

Resolving **Conflict**

I speak in many different settings and I often wear a microphone so the people in the back of a large auditorium can hear me. For the microphone to work properly, I am dependent on the person running the sound system.

Once while teaching at a large conference, the speakers started popping and hissing every time I spoke. Maybe there was interference from another room or maybe my voice sounded like it was echoing. When that happens, I've got a problem.

So at the next break I decide to talk with Larry, the guy running the sound board. Now there are two ways I could handle this conversation. I could discuss the *what*, the reverberation and the other noises; or I could discuss the *who*, which in this case is Larry. As I walked toward the sound booth, I thought about the who. *Why is it that this guy can't get it worked out? If he's a professional, shouldn't he know what he is doing? Why did I get the worst sound guy at the whole conference?*

But I knew I needed to focus on the *what*. At times like this, talking to myself can be a good thing. So as I walked toward the booth, I said to myself, "Keep it on the what. Just stay on the what. Don't go there, don't go there. Nope, nope, don't go there. Stay on the what. Keep the conversation on the what." I told myself this because I knew that as long as I could keep the conversation on the what—in this case, the sound problem—I would get the resolution I wanted. But if I moved from the what to the who (Larry), I'd create a challenge; and the problem would only escalate. If this was a chronic problem with Larry, someday we would have to address the who; but this wasn't the time to do it. My goal was to get the sound system to work properly.

By the time I reached his table, I was ready to talk about the what. "Larry, what is causing the hissing and the popping? How can we fix this?"

As long as Larry also stayed on the what, we could resolve the sound problem. If he says, "It is because there is feedback from the speakers. As long as you stay behind them you'll be okay," we stay focused on the what.

> **We need to first deal with the what before we can deal with the who.**

But if Larry says, "What are you accusing me of? It's not my fault; it's your fault. You didn't listen when I told you not to walk in front of the speakers. Are you stupid or just deaf?" This response would have been toward the who—in this case, me—rather than the what; and it is likely we never would have resolved the sound problem.

Anytime someone moves from the what to the who, it gets personal and people get defensive. Instead of getting solved, the problem escalates. We need to first deal with the what before we can deal with the who.

Here's another illustration. In small churches it always seems that there is one person who has the gift of adjusting the thermostat, and he or she likes to exercise that gift during the middle of Sunday services. This happened to me at a church I led. I had an older man whose calling was to adjust the thermostat. I would be preaching on the platform in the front; and he would get up and go to the back wall, put on his glasses, study the thermostat for a minute, and then move it back and forth. During every service he would fiddle with that thermostat while I was trying to preach. He would sit down, then a few minutes later get up and start fiddling again. He did this many times each Sunday.

I realized there was no sense in going after the who, so I took care of the what. I hired an electrician and moved the thermostat to a wall behind the platform. But I left the old controls in place. So each Sunday, the brother still got up and fiddled with the controls; but he didn't change the temperature on the real thermostat. While I was preaching, I could see him messing with the placebo controls and knew he wasn't doing anything. It was hard not to laugh aloud. For two hundred dollars, I took care of the what and never had to address the who.

Always deal with the situation, and stay there for as long as possible before dealing with the person responsible. This is the opposite of what I recommend when dealing with the challenge of focus. In focus, we start with the who and then move to the what. Who is important for focus, but when it comes to conflict, we need to stay away from the who.

Dealing with **Conflict Carriers**

Sometimes the who *is* the problem. If Mary has a problem with Dewayne, and Mary has a problem with Susan, and Mary has a problem with Gaye. The problem isn't Dewayne, Susan, and Gaye; the problem is Mary. John Maxwell calls people like Mary "conflict carriers."

It doesn't matter where they go; conflict carriers create problems. Perhaps Mary is an employee who routinely disrupts the entire staff. I can go to Mary one-on-one and say, "This is totally unacceptable behavior." Then I can explain what I expect from her and tell her that if it isn't possible for her to live up to those expectations, I will have to let her go.

But before I have that conversation, I need to have a conversation in which I help her understand what she is doing, so she has an opportunity to correct her disruptive behavior. I need to try the redemptive pathway first.

However, the suggestion comes with a warning. People like

Mary can hijack a conversation because they want to talk specific issues while we want to talk about patterns of behavior. If I begin the conversation by saying, "Yesterday at the office …," immediately she will get defensive and try to give me reasons for what happened yesterday. If I say, "There was a problem between you and Allen," immediately she's going to talk about Allen.

I need to control the conversation and frame it around the larger pattern. I need to say to her, "I've noticed conflict simmering in different times and in different ways." Then I follow with, "I really don't want to talk about any specific instance, but there seems to be a pattern here. Can you help me understand what might be going on?"

I must be especially careful with the tone of my voice and eyes. The conversation needs to take place in an informal setting. Conflict carriers put their radar up if we put them into formal situations. Authority figures cause problems for conflict carriers, so never have this conversation from the other side of a desk. Make it low key, informal, friendly, and warm. Don't go in with any agenda except to understand where the person is.

Always preface the conversation by saying, "I have noticed a pattern," and describing the pattern. Plug the holes that she will use to escape by saying, "Listen, Mary, I don't want to talk about anything specific. That's not going to help us right now. But you can help me understand what might be going on." Then patiently wait to see where she takes the conversation, gently nudging her back to the pattern when she runs for the details.

Never say to a conflict carrier, "People have told me …." If I say that, she will only become defensive and argumentative. I have to take ownership and say, "*I* have noticed …" and then ask if she can help *me* understand.

She'll try another tactic, "Well, Arthur talked to you about this."

Don't go there. Keep focused. "Just help me understand; there's a pattern over here." She is most comfortable with specifics because she has information; the patterns are harder for her to defend.

If I can do this action successfully, I will have a new opportunity to get through to Mary. If I make the mistake of focusing on a specific, the conversation is over. I have to be assertive in setting up the parameters of the conversation

My friend Jennifer heard me speak on this topic, and it helped her realize she sometimes uses this pattern when communicating with her husband. Jennifer has a sales background and has terrific verbal skills. Her husband, David, is an accountant and is more comfortable with numbers. In the past, when David tried to talk to Jennifer about an issue, she would always demand that he give her a specific instance. If he could remember, he would. But soon Jennifer would interrupt. "That one doesn't count; here's why. ..." She would then run verbal circles around him, and if David persisted, she would demand another example.

Soon David would run out of examples. Since Jennifer was able to defend herself against each specific instance, she failed to see the pattern David was trying to communicate. So David would end the conversation feeling deflated, confused, and without hope of change. Jennifer left the conversation wondering what David's problem was.

Jennifer recognized she was being a conflict carrier in her marriage. She was then able to step back and reexamine her role in the conversation. Now she is open to avoiding the specifics and learning from the patterns.

However, some people will not have the spiritual maturity to receive that advice but I still believe we should try. As leaders, we need to look at ourselves in the mirror and know that we did everything we could. We want to go the second mile, and we can do that only if we're healthy. Our health comes from being secure in our setting, even if it is a remote island with three huts.

Teaching Points

1. Absence of conflict does not mean progress.
2. There is no such thing as a conflict-free zone.
3. Conflict is neither good nor bad; it simply is.
4. The benefits of conflict are:
   - Issues are fully explored.
   - Leaders look deeper into decisions to ensure they have all the information.
   - People are committed to the final decision.
   - The decision-making process is more important than the decision itself.
5. The dark side of conflict:
   - Can make us reluctant to lead.
   - Offers potential to walk away from issues because of fear.
   - Can limit our influence.
   - Makes it hard to do our jobs well.
   - Reverberates from conflict in one area through others.
   - Mistakenly subordinates our calling in an attempt to keep peace.
6. We will never be able to please everybody.
7. There will be blood on the floor; our job is to minimize it.
8. Our health determines our response to conflict.
9. The goal of conflict isn't to end it in agreement or disagreement. The goal is ongoing health.
10. We need to honestly assess our own health. When unhealthy, avoid situations that might cause conflict.
11. We can only help others be healthy after we're healthy.
12. Healthy people and healthy churches can go through conflict and heal from it.

13. God has put us in the setting where it pleases him. We need to be secure in it.
14. People get upset because they were never set.
15. When resolving conflict, concentrate on the what, not the who.
16. Moving from the what to the who escalates the problem.
17. Sometimes the who is the problem, and there isn't a what. These people are called conflict carriers.
18. Always try the redemptive pathway first.
19. Stay focused on the pattern when talking with conflict carriers. Don't allow them to hijack the conversation to talk about specifics.
20. When dealing with conflict carriers:
    - Be careful with your tone of voice and eyes.
    - Do so in an informal situation.
    - Realize authority figures cause problems for conflict carriers.

    Make conversation low key, informal, friendly, and warm. Go the second mile when trying to make conflict carriers healthy.

CHAPTER NINE

ORGANIZATIONAL CONGRUENCE

Every company has two organizational structures: The formal one is written on the charts; the other is the everyday relationship of the men and women in the organization.

—Harold S. Geneen, former chairman, ITT

When Pastor Frye took the job at First Church two years ago, he was energized by the possibilities. He had always wanted to minister in the inner city. And the church's new multipurpose building would be the perfect combination sports complex and youth center, attracting community members to the church twenty-four hours a day, seven days a week. The program started small, but Pastor Frye's vision was big.

After a few months, the elders came to him with the idea of opening a Christian school in the building. While it wasn't exactly what the pastor had planned, it was still a ministry to the community; and it was possible to use the same space for recreation on weekends and evenings. "These are good people, and they're doing good things," he said. "There is nothing wrong with what they are asking."

First Christian School opened that fall. Temporary walls

were used, so they could be taken down after school hours to accommodate other activities. But as teachers and students settled in, the walls came down less frequently. Soon school administrators complained that noise heard through the walls was disruptive to the learning process. At the next board meeting, the principal requested some modifications to the building; and they were approved. Permanent walls would be installed where the temporary ones once stood. Pastor Frye wasn't sure if he agreed with the idea, but so many people were in favor of it that he went along.

> **The leader cannot catch up to a parade that has started without him.**

A few months later Pastor Frye walked through the corridor of classrooms, and it occurred to him that his vision of a sports ministry had been replaced by a private Christian school. He didn't feel that it was the best use of his skills, and it certainly wasn't his God-given vision for the church. But what was he supposed to do?

The Organization Must Align with the
Leader's Vision and Values

Many leaders have faced similar circumstances. They joined a church or company with a vision for one thing; but over time, the vision shifted to something else. At first the leader goes along because it's not a big deal. It's all for God's good, right? But eventually a morning comes when the leader wakes up and realizes that the organization's vision is different from his own. In this situation, many leaders say, "I can adjust my vision;" and they try following the direction set by the organization.

This will never work.

The leader cannot catch up to a parade that has started without him. Even if he makes it to the front in time, how can he lead when he doesn't know where the members are going? The leader has subordinated *his* God-given vision to a group of people who are journeying elsewhere. It might be that their destination and vision is as worthy as his, but the point is: It isn't his. It isn't what God gave *him* to do.

An organization must be in line with the leader's vision and core values. If they aren't, how can he lead them? A CEO with principles can't lead a subordinate who doesn't believe in rules. A pastor can't focus if his people aren't supporting the vision he is focused on. Organizational congruence is necessary if a church or organization wants to be functional.

What Is **Organizational Congruence?**

When a leader's vision and values are aligned with the organization's goals, the congruence will be reflected in everything they do.

For example, a local Atlanta church states that one of its core values is missions. This core value is demonstrated in everything the members do. The budget shows a large percentage of their income going to missions projects. The missions department has more people than any other department. The calendar reveals that much of the scheduling is for missions-related activities. Likewise, if both children's ministry and the missions department both wanted to meet with the pastor and he had time for only one meeting, he would choose the missions department. This focus demonstrates organizational congruence.

Another example is a business that boasts their focus is on customer service. To check, I would look at their personnel files to see how many people actually worked with customers. I would review their training and see what they are paid. I would look at all the ways customers contact the business and then see who handles those contacts and in what order of priority. I would also look to see how they treat their employees because if morale is high and conflict is low, they can serve the customer better. Customer service is either a priority or it isn't. If it is, everything about the corporation should demonstrate it as seen in the Ritz-Carlton example mentioned in an earlier chapter.

Organizational congruence begins with our focus; it flows from our vision, mission, and core values; and permeates every area of our organization. If it doesn't, we don't have congruence.

Promote Congruence through the
Use of Strategic Planning

Pastor Jones wants to grow the children's ministry at his church. This is in line with the vision of the church, which is "Bringing families to the church." Now the pastor could attend a meeting and say, "I have a vision for growing our children's ministry." But as we learned earlier, that statement is too abstract. Instead, he needs to put some concreteness behind his words. One way to do this is through strategic planning.

Pastor Jones calls his team together and says, "There are a lot of children in the apartments and buildings near the church. Let's strategically determine the best way to reach out to these kids."

After a brief discussion, because of Annette's previous experience in similar circumstances, the team looked to her to lead and coordinate this outreach. At this point, the meeting could conclude with everyone wishing Annette the best. Instead, this is the time to get strategic about implementing the proposed plan. During the meeting, take time to discuss and then write down the details of who, what, why, where, when, and how; and keep the list for future reference. To make this planning job easier, I've created a Strategic Planning Worksheet that you can photocopy and use as a guide during these kinds of meetings. Completing this worksheet during the meeting can help put details to the vision.

Strategic Planning Worksheet

1. What is our vision?

   _____

2. Why are we doing this? How does it relate to our core values?

   _____

   _____

3. Who is responsible? What will they do?

   _____

   _____

4. How do we plan to do this? (Be specific.)

   a. _____

   b. _____

   c. _____

   d. _____

   e. _____

5. When will this be done? What are the due dates for specific tasks, and who will accomplish them?

   _____

   _____

6. How much will this cost? Do we have the capacity (people, facilities, finances, etc.) to undertake this right now?

   _____

   _____

7. To whom are we accountable for this?

   _____

   _____

8. How will we measure success?

   _____

   _____

After Pastor Jones shared his vision for a comprehensive children's ministry, someone asked, "Why are we doing this?"

"Because over 70 percent of the local families have children; and if we can reach the children, we can reach the rest of their families."

"Who is going to do it?"

"Annette Ryan, our children's coordinator, will be responsible for doing it."

"How will she do it?"

"She is going to use a programming plan that worked at a church in another city."

"How much will it cost?"

"Each program will have a deadline and a budget associated with it."

"Who will she be accountable to?"

"She will report directly to me. We will evaluate her progress quarterly and base it on the growth in the number of children enrolled in Sunday school and Vacation Bible School. We also plan to have an annual review, and we will attach separate goals for that review."

Once the staff is familiar with strategic planning details, the questions and answers will fly from different parts of the room until the terms of a concrete plan are agreed on. That's the beauty of teaching strategic planning to the staff. Soon they will be doing it without realizing they are doing it.

> In most organizations, reorganizing the structure won't make people work better or harder.

Remember, this isn't a worksheet to help the team make decisions. I covered decision-making questions in an earlier chapter. What we're doing now is making sure the decisions we've already made will be strategically implemented. Taking time to put meat on the bones of an idea will help to ensure that something actually gets done. When things start to change, transitions will be easier, conflict will be reduced, and organizational congruence will increase.

This worksheet also helps to ensure that there is congruence between the people and the structure of an organization. Not only do we have to make sure that our vision and the organization are in alignment, we also need to make sure that we align people within the organizational structure, so they can create results.

People Take Precedence **Over Structure**

When things aren't working, leaders often prefer to change the formal structure of an organization because it is the easiest area to tackle. Moving boxes around on an organizational chart, reassigning who reports to whom, and handing out new titles doesn't require much management ability. It is a clean process. It is logical.

In most organizations, reorganizing the structure won't make people work better or harder. It is like the man who needs to clean out his garage but decides to organize his bedroom closet because it is easier. It may be easier, but the results won't be a cleaner garage.

Changing the formal structure won't change an individual's motivation, behavior, or imbedded mindset. We can have Mary report to Beth; but if Mary doesn't like Beth, she will continue to seek approval and guidance from her old supervisor. It might make sense to put Mark in charge of organizing volunteers because he knows how the scheduling program works. But if Mark prefers computers to people and is unable to recruit the needed help, there may be fewer volunteers. What's really important isn't the formal details of the job, it's the people in the job.

To change things in an organization, adjustments must be

made to the informal connections, not the formal structure. These informal processes and behaviors can be troublesome, but when handled properly, the results are worth the effort.

Larry Bossidy, chairman and CEO of Honeywell, said, "People have told me I spend too much time on people but I

> **People must take priority over structure.**

know that if I get the best people, I am going to walk away with the prize. In this day and age, organizations that don't have the best people don't win." People must take priority over structure.

Pastor Frye needs to understand that it isn't about a Christian school or a community recreation program. Nor is it about keeping people in-line. Rather it is keeping alignment between people, vision, and structure. Congruence is getting all the parts to work as one body. For good.

Teaching Points

1. An organization must be aligned with the leader's vision and values.
2. When out of alignment, many leaders say, "I can adjust." But doing so will never work.
3. The leader cannot catch up to a parade that started without him. Even if he makes it to the front in time, how can he lead when he doesn't know where the people are going?
4. The leader has subordinated his God-given vision to a group of people who are journeying elsewhere.
5. When seeking congruence, the group must realign with the leader's vision and core values.
6. When there is congruence, it will be reflected in everything (budget, personnel, calendar, meetings, etc.).
7. Promote congruence through the use of strategic planning.

8. Strategic planning involves detailed answers to the following kinds of questions:
    - What is our vision?
    - Why are we doing this?
    - How does it relate to our core values?
    - Who is responsible? What will they do?
    - How do we plan to do this? (Be specific.)
    - When will this be done? What are the due dates for specific tasks, and who will accomplish them?
    - How much will this cost? Do we have the capacity (people, facilities, finances, etc.) to undertake this right now?
    - To whom are we accountable for this?
    - How will we measure success?

9. People take precedence over structure. Leaders prefer to change the formal structure because it is easier than changing people. Reorganizing the structure won't bring people into alignment. To be effective, changes must be made to the informal connections, not the formal structure.

Strategic Planning Grid

WHAT	WHY	WHO	HOW	WHEN	HOW MUCH	ACCOUNTABLE TO WHOM	EVALUATION PROCESS

CHAPTER TEN

FINANCIAL MANAGEMENT

How is a pastor, trained in theology, supposed to manage a business?

—Sam Chand

W hen I first became the president of Beulah Heights Bible College, I didn't even know what an audit looked like. I had never seen one before. I didn't understand what restricted or unrestricted funds were, I had no idea what depreciation was, and the various categories of numbers made no sense at all to me. The first time I was presented with an audit, it was page after page of nothing but numbers. At the bottom of the page, in tiny print, were a lot of disclaimers. They were written in some sort of accountant-speak.

Leaders are Unprepared for **Church Finance Issues**

Most pastors in the pulpit today need to learn more about hiring, firing, personnel issues, money management, insurance, and legal responsibilities. Yet these same pastors are serving as the CEOs of multimillion-dollar corporations with major real estate holdings and employing scores of full and part-time employees. Despite our lack of training in these areas, we still are required to conform to the laws and regulations of governing bodies: Occupational Safety and Health Administration (OSHA), generally accepted accounting procedures (GAAP), Federal Deposit Insurance Corporation (FDIC), and the Internal Revenue Service (IRS), as well as health inspectors, lending laws, local ordinances, and zoning regulations.

Pastors are overwhelmed, and they should be. They didn't get the training they needed to succeed at their jobs because, until recently, seminaries didn't offer courses in business management. Due to recent corporate accounting scandals, even businesses are now facing more financial and legal scrutiny then ever before.

Churches have always been scrutinized. Members want to track how much money comes in and where it is spent, and rightfully so. The IRS watches to ensure that churches follow all of the rules to maintain their nonprofit status. Due to the neglect or downright criminal activities of some radio and TV ministers, those churches with a media ministry feel especially nervous. News reporters wanting to increase ratings use hidden camera investigations to show hypocritical religious leaders bilking money from the faithful. All of this attention causes honest leaders additional anxiety as they seek to do what's right. While these policing organizations are necessary and even good, sometimes the intimidation factor can keep good people from doing what they were called to do. How is a pastor, trained in theology, supposed to manage a business?

Leaders need to understand that they don't have the necessary expertise, and they can't get it quickly enough. Pastors are theologically prepared to serve their people, but they have no concept of how to navigate the massive amounts of financial and legal issues that are critical to running a business. They also don't have the time to learn on the job because mistakes can be costly. If there were a twelve-step financial plan for pastors, the first step would be to admit that we don't know it all and that is okay. There isn't room in today's business climate to "fake it until you make it."

Ask for Help **when Needed**

When the audit was presented to me, I didn't know how to decipher the information, so I did the only thing I could do: I asked for help. I created a presidential advisory team who met once a month to discuss finances. On the team were nine people with different backgrounds. Some of them had experience in finance or accounting, others were nonfinancial people who used the data to make decisions. This team would meet, look at the information, discuss it, and make recommendations based on their education, experience, and insight. This allowed me to make good decisions based on information that no one had ever taught me to understand.

The first thing I learned was that the most important number could be found on page three. (For other organizations, the number may be on a different page, so don't take my advice too literally.) Once I found that number, I checked to see if it had parentheses around it. If so, it was a negative number. That was bad. If not, it was a positive number; and that was good. Soon I became a financial expert and could flip open the audit and look for the parentheses, though obviously that wasn't enough information to make informed decisions.

So I learned that I had to depend on my team. I had to be healthy enough to say, "I don't understand this," or "I don't know that; can you explain it to me?"

I learned to bring different kinds of people together.

For example, staff members at the church don't regularly attend board meetings; but it makes sense for the accountant to meet with the financial committee, so she can respond to questions. Likewise, when a salesperson wants to sell the church a new security or investment plan, rather than meeting only with the pastor, everyone involved in finances at the church should be invited. If more churches were managed this way, they might not have fallen for a scheme like the one that recently bilked millions out of hundreds of churches in the Southeast.

> Refuse good advice and watch your plans fail; take good counsel and watch them succeed.
> -Proverbs 15:22 (MSG)

The Bible says that there is safety in the multitude of good counsel. Proverbs 15:22 says, "Refuse good advice and watch your plans fail; take good counsel and watch them succeed" (MSG). This is especially true in the case of financial counsel. One trusted and knowledgeable advisor isn't enough; seek financial advice from several qualified people with different backgrounds and personalities to ensure unbiased feedback.

As leaders, we are always involved in the decisions, but the role we play may change when it comes to financial or legal matters. For example, when there is a big real estate deal at the church, we're part of that decision; but we're there as a visionary, not a pragmatist. There's nothing wrong with a visionary being involved, but at the end of the deal the pragmatists will rule. They are the ones to fill out the paperwork and double check the calculations that go on the forms. We can enhance our own abilities immediately by getting other people to help us.

Choose Advisors Who Can **Give More Than Data**

Some of our advisors may be paid, and some not paid; but

the same principles that apply to selecting ladder holders also apply to the advisors we select. But it is important to maintain a balance too. When the organization reaches a certain size, having an accountant on staff is important. As we grow larger, it becomes

> **Good Advisors Give Us**
> 1. Data.
> 2. Implications of the data.
> 3. Recommendations on the implications.
> 4. Strategies for the recommendations.

important to have a paid, independent accountant available for external audits and some financial reporting.

We want to find a balance between people we are close enough to that we can pick up the phone and call for a quick question and those who are distant enough to have an independent, outside opinion.

Some leaders say, "We can't afford the financial or legal help we need." If an organization can't afford it, the leaders shouldn't be doing it because they will pay for it one way or another. Spending $50,000 a year for good legal or financial advice isn't much to pay if it could ultimately save us from five million dollars in penalties or, worse, jail time.

Good advisors give us four items in this order:

1. Data. They tell us the information.

2. Implications of the data. They explain what the data means to us. It is the context that helps us create meaning out of the information.

3. Recommendations on the implications. The advisor believes this is the best advice she can offer us based on the information and its meaning.

4. Strategies for the recommendations, The who, what, why, how, and when of implementing a chosen recommendation.

Let's see how each of these steps are used in a church. For example, our church normally takes in $100,000 in offerings each month. This past month we took in $130,000. This is the data. Dean, our accountant, comes to my office and gives me this information. But he should also give me the implications of the data. In this case Dean might say, "We can use this extra income to catch up on bills that we owe, expand a program, or save it." He might also discuss his concerns that giving could drop off next month due to vacations or additional data that suggests that church members will consistently give at this level in the future. What Dean is doing is creating meaning out of the data.

But good advisors don't stop there. Dean should state which recommendation he thinks is best, based on the information he has. "Pastor, I think we should use this additional income to pay down our debt. We've recently incurred higher utility bills; and with the interest on the debt, I am afraid that if we don't reduce our monthly expenses, we will exceed our budget for the year." He then presents the data that makes up his recommendation.

If Dean has done his job, we will have all the information we need, as well as the context for understanding that information. The recommendations made can help us think through the available choices and compare our thoughts with those of the advisor. Then we can make a decision.

Normally at this point Dean would say, "Okay, let me make a plan based on your decision and get back with you in a few days." Instead, we need to train our advisors to have a plan *before* the meeting. If Dean has four recommendations, he needs to come to the meeting with all four plans in place. So when I say, "I want to do one and three," the strategies for one and three are already laid out. If the plan is already in place, Dean can act on it as soon as I decide. He doesn't waste time trying to figure out what to do next. The phone numbers, dollar amounts, or forms that need to be signed are already organized and ready to go.

Let's say that the pastor decides he wants to take the extra $30,000 and divide it between two projects. He wants to use

$20,000 for a new playground for the children and he wants to donate $10,000 to world hunger. Without a plan in place, Dean will have to go figure out who sells play sets, for how much, and where on the campus the new playground should be installed. Then he will have to determine which missions agencies provide food relief and which countries those organizations serve. Should the money be designated towards one agency serving one country or one agency serving multiple countries? Maybe it should be divided between multiple agencies.

A capable secretary can count money and figure out that we took in $30,000 more than usual. But financial counselors should provide their leaders with the meaning by putting the data into context. They should present specific recommendations, so together we can arrive at the best solution and then act on it. If Dean comes to the meeting with these plans in place, we can immediately execute the plan once we determine the decision.

We need to encourage the people who work for us to come up with multiple solutions and then strategies for implementing each of those solutions. Demanding this kind of information and strategic planning from the people who work for us is one way to develop them as leaders. This is a practical example of how we can help raise the ceiling. By expecting more information from them than they are currently giving, we can help them raise their leadership ceiling.

Financial **Don'ts**

Don't let advisors decide. A leader should always be the one to make the final decision. The information should be presented and even discussed by a team of financial counselors but we should never abdicate our decision-making power. If we don't have the information we need, we can request that the advisors do more research, get new advisors, or ask more questions.

Regardless, we must take responsibility for the decision. Vision and ultimate decision making are two things a leader should never delegate.

Don't get compromised. Many leaders start out as principled decision-makers, but in an effort to make numbers look more appealing to their stakeholders, they begin to make decisions based on situations. Don't let circumstances guide financial decisions. Always make decisions based on principle, regardless of the immediate consequences. The long-term consequences of situational decision making will always be worse than the immediate cost.

> **Vision and ultimate decision making are two things a leader should never delegate.**

Don't try to do everything. If I can help leaders understand one thing, it would be that they don't have to do everything. This is especially true in areas where they may be ill equipped to do the job, such as financial management.

Do What You **Do Best**

In Acts 6, the Grecian widows were complaining that they were not getting their food. The Apostles agreed that it was a legitimate complaint, but they also knew it was outside of their calling. So the Twelve arranged a meeting and asked all the disciples to attend.

I can imagine one of them getting up at the meeting and saying something like this: "The widows are complaining again, and they've got a legitimate gripe. There has been some mismanagement going on, and we don't have the time or skills to make sure this is getting done and getting done right. My focus is on spreading the Good News, preparing people for the second coming, and leading people spiritually. Food distribution isn't really my forte. I don't know much about Meals on Wheels. I don't have any experience in purchasing bulk ingredients, food preparation, or timely distribution of meals."

According to Acts, the Apostles then decided to appoint people to handle these actions for them. From all those attending the meeting, they asked the group to select seven who met these criteria: the men must be honest, filled with the Holy Spirit, and have good sense. Essentially, they wanted people who were qualified to handle the responsibility.

Once the men were selected, they ran the food program, so the Apostles could concentrate on other things. Obviously, they must have picked the right people because the problem seemed to have disappeared after that meeting.

There is a big difference between understanding *ministry* and understanding the *business of ministry*. Most church leaders are not equipped to direct the business of ministry. Their lack of education and experience in this area makes them a liability rather than an asset. In these cases, the best information comes from trusted advisors who aren't afraid to teach us what they already know. They are ultimately the ones who can provide us with the information we need to make the best decisions. That's why I recommend that leaders spend less time concerned about their audit trail and more time concerned about their information trail.

Teaching Points

1. Most leaders are unprepared for financial issues.
2. Pastors don't have business training, yet they are called to serve as CEOs of multimillion-dollar corporations.
3. Leaders don't have the time to learn on the job, and mistakes are costly.
4. We need to admit that we don't know it all.
5. We need to be healthy enough to ask for help when we need it.
6. Good counsel is found in a multitude of advisors.
7. When bringing advisors together:
   - Look for people with different backgrounds to give a greater perspective.
   - Look for the same characteristics found in good ladder holders.
   - Look for a balance between people with whom we can pick up the phone and call at anytime and those we pay for an independent, outside opinion.
   - Look for those who aren't afraid to tell us the truth.
8. If our organizations can't afford to pay for needed counsel, we shouldn't be doing what it is we're doing because we will pay for it one way or another.
9. Good advisors give us:
   - Data.
   - Implications of the data.
   - Recommendations on the implications.
   - Strategies for the recommendations.
10. Demanding this kind of information and strategic planning from the people who work for us is one way for us to help them develop as leaders.
11. Financial don'ts include the following:
    - Don't let advisors decide.

- Don't get compromised.
- Vision and ultimate decision making are two actions that a leader should never delegate.
- Don't try to do everything.

12. Leaders should do what they do best. The rest should be given to qualified people we designate, just as the Apostles did in Acts 6.

13. There is a big difference between understanding ministry and understanding the business of ministry.

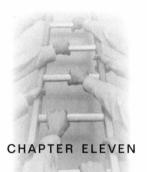

CHAPTER ELEVEN

TIME ALLOCATION

*Avoiding the phrase "I don't have time …," will soon
help you to realize that you do have the time needed for just
about anything you choose to accomplish in life.*

—Bo Bennett, author of Year to Success

Cassandra always had a flair for decorating. She loved to
help her friends pick out paint and wallpaper, and she always
knew where to find the best deals on furniture and accessories.
When Cassandra helped Susan decorate her house, Susan suggested that Cassandra start her own business. With Susan's
encouragement, Cassandra's Home Interiors was born.

At first Cassandra loved it. She had always enjoyed coordi-
nating fabrics and paint, and now she was getting paid to do it.
As people saw her work, the demand for her services grew. She
often spent long hours working after the kids were in bed, but
she was energized by her success and appreciated the extra
money.

Then things began to change. Cassandra used to meet her
kids at the bus stop everyday. But as her business grew and she
needed the extra time, she enrolled them in an after-school

program until their dad could get off work and pick them up. With her busy schedule, she no longer had time to cook. She began to pick up fast-food meals on the way home from appointments and then let the kids watch TV in their rooms while she worked on billing.

Instead of energizing her, the long hours began to wear on her; but she had to continue working. She had invested money in the business, buying a new computer, carrying an inventory of popular accessories, and upgrading her old car to a new SUV. The new car gave her a competitive edge because she could now deliver small pieces of furniture and custom drapery rods herself. As her expenses increased, it was more important than ever that Cassandra continue to take on new clients, so she could pay her bills.

> **What started out as fun now owns me.**

Soon the only time Cassandra had available to show fabrics was in the evenings and on weekends. What started out as fun began to compete with the important things in her life like time with her family. Cassandra knew her family should come first, and that's truly what she wanted. But the extra income helped them to pay for things they couldn't afford before, like the new car and a vacation. Of course, they couldn't actually go on a vacation because Cassandra couldn't take that much time off. What was she supposed to do? If she cut back, she couldn't afford the car payments; but if she kept up that business pace, she was going to lose her family. When discussing her predicament with Susan, Cassandra remarked, "What started out as fun now owns me."

Avoiding **Burnout**

We've all had that experience where something that started

out as invigorating soon became something we dreaded doing. How did it happen? My guess is that it happens to us the same way it happened to Cassandra. What we started for fun took on a life of its own. It grew bigger than the hobby stage and became something that overtook the rest of our lives.

Someone once described burnout as something that happens "when you stop doing what you love to do to engage in the activities that support doing what you love." In order for Cassandra to have fun picking out fabrics and wallpaper, she had to solicit new clients, make deliveries, spend time writing up estimates, and billing clients. Soon she was spending more time doing the things that supported her talents than she spent using her talents.

The same thing happens in a church when a young minister is excited about finally being able to fulfill his calling. After a few years on the job, he discovers he is spending more time dealing with personnel then he is in the pulpit. His day is filled with meetings, but he isn't doing much ministry. Burnout sets in quickly because he isn't doing what energizes him. He is doing what he has to do to keep the collection plates full and the congregation happy.

We love to pursue our passions and yet we know we must do the other things too. As leaders, we try to make up for this imbalance by working longer and harder. Ultimately, our resources are limited. We only have twenty-four hours in a day. An unhealthy lifestyle and a lack of sleep will eventually catch up with us. Something has to give.

Defining **Priorities**

When we started out, we could be everywhere and do everything. We worked eighteen-hour days; and though they were long days, we got a lot done. We had unlimited energy and vision. But as the organization grew, more demands were made on our time. The list kept getting longer, but nothing ever got checked off.

To regain control over our time, we have to start with our priorities. In many ways, this goes back to understanding focus as discussed in the first chapter. But defining our priorities goes beyond our focus at work to include what is important in our lives. Our focus at work may be to finish a building campaign, but our priority in life might be our relationships with God and then with our family. Regardless of how much paperwork there is for the new construction, if God is a priority, spending time with him comes first. If family is a priority, then choose little Tommy's T-ball game over the 7:00 meeting with the builders. The contractor can wait until tomorrow.

Every yes is pregnant with a no.

The ability to make these kinds of decisions is evidence that we have defined our priorities. An inability to make these decisions indicates we're unclear about what comes first in our lives.

I once heard someone say that every yes is pregnant with a no. When I say yes to attend my son's game, I must say no to being present at the late meeting at church. When I say yes to working weekends, I must say no to spending time with my family. Defining priorities means I am clear on what is a yes and what is a no.

In his book, *Choosing to Cheat: Who Wins when Family and Work Collide?* Andy Stanley says that cheating is "the decision to give up one thing in order to gain something else." Usually there is a negative connotation associated with the word. We think of cheating on our taxes as a way to get a few extra dollars, but we rarely consider that we're giving up our integrity to do so. When a woman cheats on her husband, she is giving up her fidelity for a few minutes of hedonistic pleasure.

But Stanley says that we are all cheaters. We all trade one thing for another. He rightly points out that we could work twenty-four hours a day, seven days a week and not get it all done. Likewise, we could give up our jobs to stay home with the family and still wouldn't hear the kids say, "I am done playing, Dad; you can go back to work now." Or hear our wives say, "That's enough, Honey; you've helped me so much. I have nothing left to do."

At some point, we cheat work to go home to our families even though there are phone calls to be made, e-mails to be answered, and paperwork to finish. We also cheat our families by saying, "I'll get to the next game," or "Don't wait up; I'll be late." Since we can't get more time, Stanley recommends that we decide right now that we will say no to work and yes to our families, making them our first priority. He advocates cheating on work, so we can spend more time with the family.

In that book, Stanley uses several examples of executives who find a way to break away from their work for days or even weeks when there is a crisis at home. When a spouse or child gets sick or there is an emergency, we all find it easy to say, "I've got to go now." But we rarely have that kind of confidence without a crisis. If family is a priority, we must learn to say yes to them and be pregnant with a no to things that aren't a priority.

Put Things in the **Right Order**

But the question remains: How do we maximize our time? Instead of pedaling faster and still not going as far as we want to go, how do we make it all work? Consider this example. A large empty Plexiglas® transparent tank sits on the table next to four large buckets. One bucket is filled with water, the second with sand, the third with gravel, and the last bucket is filled with rocks. The buckets are only slightly smaller than the tank. "I need someone to fill this tank, using everything in these buckets," the instructor announces.

A student comes forward. She pours in the water and some of the sand until the tank is nearly full. She tries to add some gravel and a few rocks. But she can't do so without the contents of the tank spilling over the top. "Keep trying until you can get everything from the buckets into the tank," encourages the instructor. The task looks impossible. After trying and failing several times, the student thinks she may have a solution. She tests it.

First, she puts the largest rocks into the tank. Next, she puts in the gravel. The gravel fills in the spaces around the big rocks, leaving her room to put in the sand. The sand fills in all the corners and crevices until the tank looks nearly full, yet there is still room for the water. She pours it in, leaving the buckets empty and the tank full. She had found a way to accomplish what looked to be an impossible task.

As leaders, our days are often overscheduled with not nearly enough time to get it all done. Our to-do lists taunt us with their unattainable goals. When we see a demonstration like this, we're tempted to think that the lesson is: If we try hard enough, we can squeeze it all in. But that isn't the point. The message behind this illustration is that we must always start with the big rocks. If we don't start with the big rocks, we will never fit in everything else. However, once the big rocks are in place, there is always room for the little things.

The big rocks are our priorities. If we put the priorities in first, we can make the other things fit. When Cassandra's decorating was a hobby and her family came first, she had time for them *and* time to do what she loved. Now that she is supposedly doing what she loves, she doesn't have time for either. The tank represents our lives and the time that it holds. What is important is the order, or the priority, of the items we place in our tanks, not the amount we can squeeze into it.

Schedule Your **Priorities**

To be able to put the big things in first, we need to know what they are. As leaders, we need to be as clear about our priorities as we are about our focus. Once we know what our priorities are, we need to decide how we will deal with interruptions. If a yes to a priority means a no to something else, we need to communicate why we're choosing one over the other to people whose priorities may differ from ours. Once we've got a handle on what is and isn't a priority, we can maximize our days by scheduling our priorities.

> Todd Duncan of the Duncan Group says that it is not about prioritizing our schedules; it is about scheduling our priorities.

Todd Duncan of the Duncan Group says that it is not about prioritizing our schedules; it is about scheduling our priorities. What he means is that we need to proactively make decisions to honor our priorities. Just as the student figured out she needed to put the big rocks in first, we need to decide what the priorities are and schedule those. The alternative is reacting to whatever happens during the day, which will ultimately lead to cheating on our priorities.

Time allocation isn't about finding more time or squeezing more in. It is about being deliberate. It is about intentionally giving time to the things that are a priority. We all have the same amount of time, but we each get to choose how we allocate it. To paraphrase Andy Stanley, when managing time, choose to cheat. Don't cheat on the priorities.

Teaching Points

1. If we're not deliberate, what starts out as fun can eventually own us.

2. Burnout happens when we stop doing what we love to do to engage in the activities that support doing what we love. For example, spending more time in meetings rather than in ministry leads to burnout.

3. In the beginning, we can work long hours with unlimited vision and energy. As the organization grows, we also grow the list of demands on our time.

4. We must define our priorities.

5. Priorities go beyond our focus at work to include what's important in our lives.

6. Every yes is pregnant with a no. We can't say yes to something without saying no to something else.

7. Andy Stanley, in his book Choosing to Cheat: Who Wins when Family and Work Collide? says that cheating is "the decision to give up one thing, in order to gain something else."

8. We are all cheaters; but we need to be deliberate cheaters and choose to cheat on work, not on family.

9. If we can find time to get away from work during a family crisis, we can find time when there isn't a crisis.

10. To do this, we need to put our priorities in the right order.

11. It is a myth to think that if we just try hard enough, we can squeeze it all in.

12. We must always start with the big rocks (our priorities). If we don't start with the big rocks, we will never be able to get them in our lives. However, once the big rocks are taken care of, there is always room for the little things.

13. Putting our priorities first can open up space for the other things to fit. Todd Duncan of the Duncan Group says that it is not about prioritizing our schedules, it is about scheduling our priorities.

14. Good time allocation is about being deliberate. It is about intentionally allocating it according to our priorities.

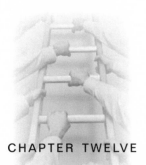

CHAPTER TWELVE

CONTROL VS. DELEGATION

*Surround yourself with the best people you can find,
delegate authority, and don't interfere.*

—Ronald Reagan, fortieth President of the United States

As president of Beulah Heights Bible College, I was like most leaders. I was in the unenviable position of being able to choose my own pain. Specifically, that meant that when an important project came up, I could choose to do it myself; or I could delegate it to someone else. Either option caused me pain.

Doing it myself typically meant working long hours and letting other responsibilities slip as I roughed my way through the task alone. After doing this a few times, it didn't take long for me to realize that I couldn't do everything by myself. Other aspects of my job didn't get the attention they needed as I focused my energy on the project. And my family suffered because I had to spend more time at work.

But at the time, delegating jobs to other people didn't seem like a better option. When I did everything myself, I knew it would get done exactly the way I wanted it. But if I delegated that responsibility, I had no assurance of the outcome. There were more questions than answers. What if she doesn't do the job the way I would? What if her performance isn't up to my standards? What if she completely fails and I still have to do it? Not only would I still have to get the job done on time, but now I would have even less time in which to do it.

> For leaders who are used to being in charge, this means a new type of pain: the pain of delegating.

That's why I say it was an unenviable position. I could choose between the pain of doing it myself and the pain of delegating it.

Delegating **Difficulties**

As our organization continues to grow, there comes a time when we learn that we can't do it all ourselves. For leaders who are used to being in charge, this means a new type of pain: the pain of delegating.

Baby boomers are used to being in control, so delegating can be hard for people like us. The more I delegate, the more out of control I am; and the greater the opportunity there is for something to go wrong. Delegating can cause conflict, disappointment, and discouragement; ultimately it could still mean that I end up doing it myself.

That's why we often hear leaders say, "If I want it done right, I'll just do it myself." We like the feeling of control that comes from knowing that we rise or fall based on our own actions. Yet control can camouflage pain, the pain associated with doing it ourselves. We can't do it all alone, other aspects of our work and family life suffer, and we never live up to our perfectionist tendencies.

We may choose to go it alone; yet when we're in the situation, we complain there is never anyone to help us. The truth is, people are willing to help us; we just have to be willing to go through the pain of delegating. When a leader

> **Leaders who haven't learned to delegate are needy and clinging.**

continues to hold on long after he should have let go, it is a good sign that he is drowning. Only drowning people have a death grip, so if someone doesn't want to give up it could mean he or she is drowning.

Avoid people who can't let go. Drowning victims will try to take their rescuers down with them in their desperate struggles to hang on. Leaders who haven't learned to delegate are needy and clinging. They will drown themselves in their inability to delegate to others.

All leaders have the same opportunity I had as president of the college; we can trade one kind of pain for another. Either we do tasks ourselves, or we delegate them.

Pain Threshold **Determines Height**

The more pain you can handle as a leader, the higher you will go. By learning to delegate and surviving the associated pain, we widen our bases and expand our horizons. For example, if I am the only person who can approve check requests, I must go through each request before a check can be issued. Occasionally, a vendor needs a check immediately to ensure a discount or certain delivery deadline. In order for that vendor to get his check, I must stop whatever I am doing and review the request, authorize it, and then ask the accountant to prepare the check.

I could delegate this responsibility to my assistant. If I do so, I know she is likely to make mistakes. Some of those mistakes could be costly. But if I don't delegate, I will continue to be interrupted to review check requests, even while I am working on more important things.

A leader will only grow to the threshold of his pain. In other words, I won't allow my assistant to review check requests unless

> **A leader will only grow to the threshold of his pain.**

I am willing to go through the pain of teaching her and watching her fail. If I make it through that pain, I have someone else to review the check requests; and I no longer have to deal with interruptions. I can do more and do it with greater concentration now that I have delegated another responsibility.

Ultimately, a leader's rise is dependent on the amount of pain he can handle. If we insist on staying in control, our organizations can grow no larger than our own abilities. But if we learn to delegate and then do it over and over again, we expand the base of our organization. Of course, the only way to grow the organization is to expand the base.

IBM does an excellent job of this. Leaders continually delegate responsibilities and educate employees. They understand that some employees will leave after they've been trained and use their new skills elsewhere. Instead of alienating or ignoring former employees, they embrace them. Once the employee takes

> **If we insist on staying in control, our organizations can grow no larger than our own abilities.**

another job, IBM invites him back to join the IBM alumni association. As a result, many of IBM's old employees become new customers purchasing products and services and serving as positive mouthpieces in the marketplace.

While the individual manager may feel the loss of an individual employee, the company as a whole doesn't feel it. IBM has a long-term vision. Leaders at IBM realize that the training and experiences received while employed by IBM will continue to serve the company's goals even if the employee no longer works for IBM. When a client contract needs to be negotiated or there is a new sales opportunity, IBM managers can contact former employees who are now working for customers or potential customers.

> **The only solution to the pain of delegation is the three Ds: Discover, Develop, and Deploy.**

In this way, IBM not only grows its base internally, but it grows it externally as well. Many organizations will never grow because they don't see the advantages of growing the base.

The Antidote **to Pain**

The only solution to the pain of delegation is the three Ds: Discover, Develop, and Deploy. I *discover* that Chuck has many of the leadership qualities we discussed earlier. I decide that I will *develop* him as a leader and spend a lot of time helping him grow. But I can't stop there. At some point I have to stop developing and start trusting that he is ready to take on his own responsibilities. I need to start delegating things to Chuck, I need to *deploy* him as a leader. The last thing I want to do is raise a leader and then try to sit on him. Yet that is why many good people have been forced to leave their churches or

> **The last thing I want to do is raise a leader and then try to sit on him.**

businesses; the leader was not willing to deploy them. As leaders, we have to remember that the more responsibility we delegate, the higher we can go.

In chapter 11, "Time Allocation," I discussed the importance of saying no. But delegating isn't about saying no. Delegating is about saying yes to letting someone else do it. How much pain are we willing to tolerate? The answer will tell us how high we will rise as leaders.

Teaching Points

1. We choose our own pain; we do a task ourselves or we delegate it.
2. Doing it ourselves means working long hours and letting other responsibilities slip. Eventually we learn we can't do it all.
3. When we delegate a responsibility, we have no assurance of the outcome.
4. Delegating is a loss of control. The more out of control we are, the greater the opportunity for something to go wrong.
5. We may choose to go it alone, yet we complain there is never anyone to help us. People are willing to help us; we have to be willing to go through the pain of delegating.
6. When a leader continues to hold on long after he should have let go, it is a good sign that he is drowning.
7. Avoid people who can't let go. Drowning victims will instinctively try to take their rescuers down with them.
8. A leader will only grow to the threshold of his pain. The more pain he can handle as a leader, the higher he will go as a leader.
9. If we learn to delegate and then do it over and over again, we expand the base of our organization.
10. The only solution to the pain of delegation is the three Ds:
    - Discover new leaders.
    - Develop them as leaders.
    - Deploy them to lead others.

CHAPTER THIRTEEN

EXECUTION

It is not always what we know or analyze before we make a decision that makes it a great decision. It is what we do after we make the decision to implement and execute it that makes it a good decision.

—C. William Pollard, chairman and CEO of the
ServiceMaster Company

The luncheon was extremely important to Linda. It would be her first chance to address the movers and shakers in her community with her plans for revitalizing the downtown area. She had carefully planned the details of the meeting and her staff had faithfully executed them. Or so she thought.

On her way to the meeting, she learned that the CEOs of three of the largest local businesses hadn't even been invited. After consulting with her assistant, she learned that everyone was scheduled to arrive at 12:00, but the caterer wouldn't arrive until 12:30. Now she would have to come up with a filler for thirty minutes and make it look like it was part of the program. It also meant that she would have to deliver her speech while people were eating, so she could get it in before the guests had to return to their offices.

Linda was furious. It appeared that her staff had not lived up to her expectations. This wasn't at all what she had planned.

Expectations vs. **Reality**

We can have all the staff meetings we want, but we won't get anything accomplished unless someone actually does something. Linda had certain expectations about how the luncheon would be handled, and she believed that she had communicated those to her staff. But the reality was different from what she had expected. This distance between expectations and reality is known as conflict.

Consider another example. When we hire Cynthia, we have expectations about how she will perform her work, what time she will show up in the morning, and what time she will leave. Conflict occurs when she comes in late, leaves early, or doesn't do her work in the time or way we expect.

> The distance between expectations and reality is known as conflict.

Likewise, Cynthia has expectations about how much she will be paid, how long she will work, and what she will be asked to do. Conflict occurs when she thinks she will be managing people, and instead she's asked to get coffee. Or she thinks bonuses will be based on sales, and instead they're based on longevity.

If leadership is about anything, it is about managing expectations.

Our job is to minimize the distance between expectations and reality. The closer we can bring them together, the less conflict there will be. The best way to make sure that expectations and reality match is to communicate the details clearly and concretely. In the first example, Linda may have thought she told her assistant what she wanted done for the luncheon. But as a leader Linda may have been more focused on her vision than on the details. It is possible that she communicated the information abstractly, and her assistant followed up with concrete details of her own. Unfortunately, the assistant's concrete details didn't match the details Linda envisioned.

Lack of **Execution**

I was riding in the car with a pastor of a large and prestigious church. We were talking about the growth he was experiencing when he suddenly interrupted the

> If leadership is about anything, it is about managing expectations.

conversation. "Excuse me, but I need to call the church. Your comment reminded me of something." He then used his cell phone to call the worship leader to make sure a detail was being handled for Sunday's service.

We continued the conversation, but soon it happened again. "Pardon me, I just remembered that we were supposed to respond to the zoning board today with some information it needs to consider our rezoning request. Let me just call the office, and make sure they remembered to take care of it." As we drove, our conversation was interrupted many times while the pastor made phone calls to follow up on one item or another.

Some might think the pastor was disorganized or he was trying to micromanage his people. I might have thought the same thing, but I've seen the same symptoms with many other leaders. The pastor was trying to make

> After all is said and done, more is said than done.

sure his people followed through with what they promised to do. He was following up to see that his team had done their jobs, that they had executed the plan. I see this kind of behavior in organizations all the time. After all is said and done, more is said than done.

My clients confirm this. They tell me that nothing is happening in their churches because there is a lack of implementation. They wake up in the middle of the night asking, "I wonder if that got done? Did that letter go out in today's mail? I hope she made that phone call. I wonder who is handling the details of the funeral. Did they get the contribution statements out on time?" When the pastor is out of the office, these kinds of questions swarm like mosquitoes that must constantly be swatted by phoning the office to see if they are being handled.

The leader doesn't have the peace of mind that he can delegate the details to someone else to finish. Instead, he is surrounded by people who say yes because they want the credit; but they fail to follow through. These people push the details down to the next level and hope they get done. This issue highlights the gap between the senior pastor and the next level of leadership.

> John Maxwell says, "People don't do what you expect; people do what you inspect."

The solution to this problem can be as simple as what I discussed in a previous chapter. When in a meeting, before moving from one agenda item to another, answer the question, "Who does what by when?" If this question doesn't get answered, the job is not going to get done. So when I lead meetings, I always ask *who* is going to do *what* before I move on. Then I find out *when* they will get it done.

The when is an important part of this equation. We can't forget the when. If I say, "Chris, get back to me as soon as possible," I already know that my "as soon as possible" is sooner than his "as soon as possible." When I say to someone, "Be there early," I already know that my early is earlier than his early. Unless we put a specific *when* with the *who* and the *what*, we will be frustrated. A vague when is the same as not having a when at all.

Most of us have interviewed for jobs. At the end of a meeting, the interviewer has four choices as to how to follow up. He can say:

"I'll get back to you."

"I'll get back to you next week."

"I'll get back to you next Wednesday."

"I'll get back to you next Wednesday at 10:00."

As the person who is waiting to hear back, which one would you prefer? I know I would prefer the one that was most specific. It is clear as to what will happen and when it will happen. But what if the interviewer said instead, "I will get back to you soon." Suppose another job came up on Tuesday, should I take it or not? Maybe my definition of soon was Monday.

Most high-impact leaders are shouting, "Just get it done. Make it happen!" But it is easier to make it happen when we know who is supposed to do what by when. John Maxwell says, "People don't do what you expect; people do what you inspect." Knowing who is to do it and when it is supposed to be done makes it easy for us to inspect and hold them accountable if it doesn't get done.

"The method of the enterprising is to plan with audacity and execute with vigor," said the author Christian Nestell Bovee.

The slogan for the Nike shoe company is, "Just do it!"

If leaders want to see results and avoid conflict, then I say, "Ask who will be doing what by when, and then inspect what you expect."

Teaching Points

1. We can have all the staff meetings we want, but we won't get anything accomplished unless someone actually does something.
2. If leadership is about anything, it is about managing expectations.
3. Conflict occurs when there is a difference between expectations and reality.
4. As leaders, our jobs are to minimize the distance between expectations and reality.
5. The best way to make sure that expectations and reality match is to communicate the details clearly and concretely.
6. After all is said and done, more is said than done.
   - Leaders complain that nothing is happening in their organizations because there is a lack of implementation.
   - Leaders are often surrounded by people who say yes but push the details down to the next level, hoping someone down there will do them and they can take the credit.
7. Solve the execution problem by clearly articulating the commitments at every meeting. Before moving from agenda item number one to item number two, answer the question, "Who does what by when?"
8. If this question doesn't get answered, the job is not going to get done.
9. A vague when is the same as not having a when at all.
10. People prefer the most specific details when it comes to expectations.
11. John Maxwell says, "People don't do what you expect; people do what you inspect."
12. Knowing who is to do the task and when it is supposed to be done makes it easier for us to inspect and make sure the correct person is held accountable.

CHAPTER FOURTEEN

FUTURE THINKING

The opportunity of a lifetime must be seized during the lifetime of the opportunity.

—Leonard Ravenhill, English evangelist

It was like every staff meeting at every other medium-sized church across America. First the pastor prayed. Then the finance person gave a report on what was collected and what was spent during the previous month. The education minister talked about the change in attendance, and the children's minister reported the details on the previous month's Easter egg hunt. Next month the meeting will be the same, except the children's minister will report on vacation Bible school instead of Easter.

While it may sound dull, this kind of meeting happens on a weekly or monthly basis in churches all across the country. The problem isn't that the meetings are dull. (Though they probably are.) The problem is with the focus of the meeting. These meetings only look at the past. They report what has been, not what is coming up. Leaders need to spend less time looking at the past and more time anticipating the future.

Future **Planning**

The world I was trained to minister in doesn't exist anymore. Pastors weren't taught how to prepare a sermon using multimedia, yet large screens projecting graphics, maps, Bible verses, and even videos often overshadow today's pulpits. Using a song, dance, or short drama to set up the sermon topic is also popular in many churches. The way I was trained to preach, teach, administrate, and counsel isn't effective in today's church.

Think about all the changes that have occurred in our world in the last decade. Computers have changed our lives, creating new ways to bank, shop, and travel. The proliferation of cell phones has changed how we communicate. Think of how digital and video cameras have opened up new possibilities for using images. Even our homes and churches are built differently than they were a few years ago.

Now suppose I send my first child off to kindergarten today. What will life be like for him when he graduates high school? Will he use a cell phone? Will e-mails still be around? How will he watch television? What subjects will he study in high school or college? What jobs are here today that won't be here then? Will he even leave his house to go to work?

In my book *Futuring: Leading Your Church into Tomorrow,* I suggest this is the kind of thinking that needs to be done inside our churches and organizations. We need to have extended planning sessions to get our teams to think creatively about what church will look like a few years from now. Fifteen years is too far out. I recommend teams start by looking at the next three to five years. Divide the leaders into groups, and give them questions to investigate. Ask them to report their findings in three months.

Here are some questions to get them started: Over the next three to five years, how will our church change demographically?

Will we have more male or female members? Which age group will grow the fastest? Why? What will the ethnicity, socioeconomic factors, and education of our members be like in three years? How will the neighborhoods around the church look? What developments are planned that we don't know about? Is there a plan to build a Wal-Mart, a new school, or a low-income subsidized apartment complex on land near the church? Is there a highway planned that could come through the parking lot and take three acres of our property? How will traffic flow change based on new construction patterns?

Some of this information is available from city hall, the Chamber of Commerce, or other local business bureaus. Other pieces of information can be taken from corporate cues. If McDonald's has recently moved into the neighborhood, we can assume that the corporation believes the neighborhood will be steady for the next few years. If the local McDonald's franchise builds a playground, corporate research probably shows there are a lot of growing families nearby.

Is the local school board considering a new school building? If so, educators are planning for growth in the next five to ten years. Is the school an elementary, middle, or high school? What does that tell us about growth in this area? Are there water or electrical lines being run to a certain location? Has a developer filed plans for a subdivision even though work hasn't begun on the land?

Answering these questions and others like them can help us understand how the needs of our members might be changing in the near future.

Suppose our team members come back in a few months and have found information that suggests the community around the church will be increasingly Latino. They've also learned that a subsidized housing complex will be built on the next block. Knowing this information, we can make decisions about our ministries and programming. For example, who on the staff speaks Spanish? Have we considered an English as a second language ministry? Should we add a Spanish-speaking worship service? What other services can we offer? Should we consider adding a daycare for working mothers?

Someone once said, "Opportunities are never postponed; they're lost forever." We will miss opportunities if we are not intentionally planning. Leaders need to spend more time thinking about the future and less time thinking about the past. Imagine how the staff meeting at the beginning of this chapter would be transformed if, instead of looking backward, the church began to look forward. The only thing we can do about the past is learn from it; but even so, for those lessons to be valuable, they have to be applied to the future.

> **Opportunities are never postponed; they're lost forever.**

Futuring **Leaders**

Futuring leaders forecast trends, envision scenarios, and help to create the desired future. Futuring leaders are vision driven. They say things like, "Where are we going? What are we going to do?" not, "Where have we been?" They look through the windshield while they drive, not the rearview mirror.

If we attend a meeting led by a futuring leader, the time will be spent on things that are coming up rather than things that have already been. A futuring leader intentionally applies the lessons from the past to future activities. His whole way of thinking and talking is focused on the future.

> **Futuring leaders forecast trends, envision scenarios, and help to create the desired future.**

If Bart messes up, many leaders would get on him for his mistakes. A futuring leader uses language in a different way, saying instead, "Bart, the next time you do this … ." His whole vocabulary is about the future.

Using the example of the leadership meeting above, a financial person who works for a futuring leader won't bring only reports to the monthly staff meeting. Instead, he will also bring projections. He knows that financial and strategic planning go arm in arm. Likewise, when it comes time to talk about vacation Bible school, the children's minister will only spend a few minutes debriefing about what happened this year. The focus of her time will be spent on planning for next year.

The future opens up possibilities. Furturing leaders are exciting to be around because they always see the opportunities, but we can't be futuring leaders alone. We must also take time to help our teammates learn to be future gazers and future planners.

> ## Challenges for Futuring Leaders
> If you are or seek to become a futuring leader, here are five challenges you need to face:
> 1. Focus the majority of your efforts on the future.
> 2. Understand the fundamental nature of change.
> 3. Appreciate complex systems and how they work.
> 4. Examine your leadership style.
> 5. Create a shared vision to build bridges in the future.

Past Leaders May **Not Be Future Leaders**

The leaders who got us to this point may not be the ones who carry us into the future. This is one of the hardest lessons to learn. The people who got us from 100 to 200 members may not be the ones that take us from 200 to 300. People who got us from five staff members to fifteen may not be the ones who take us from fifteen to thirty staff members. Let me say it this way: Our new leaders will rarely be our old leaders. It's not that they're incapable of leading; it's that they are incapable of seeing the organization any differently than when they came in.

When Lewis came to the church, it had 300 members. Now the church has grown to over 1,000, but he still sees it as a 300-member church and still wants to make decisions as if it were. He wants to pay the pastor a salary that's appropriate for a 300-member church, and he expects the personal touch of a 300-member church. People see things at the point they came in. It's hard for them to adjust to a new paradigm.

> **Our new leaders will rarely be our old leaders.**

We need to recruit future thinking leaders to go with us. We need people who can envision the future. Some of our original leaders won't be able to take the journey, so we need to plan for how we disengage them as leaders. This transition can be difficult, but it is necessary.

After Walt Disney's death and then the completion of Disney World, someone said, "Isn't it too bad Walt Disney didn't live to see this!" Mike Vance, creative director of Disney Studios replied, "He did see it—that's why it's here."[1]

Vance understood how Disney envisioned the future. It was Walt Disney himself who said, "The future is not the result of choices among alternative paths offered in the present—it is a place that is created—created first in the mind and will; created next in activity."[2]

As leaders, we need to have our minds on the future and have the activities to back it up.

Teaching Points

1. The world that most leaders were trained for no longer exists.
2. Consider for a minute how the world has changed in the past decade. Now consider how much it will change by the time today's kindergartners graduate from high school in 15 years. This is the kind of thinking that needs to be done inside our churches.
3. A daylong or a half-daylong planning session should be used to get the team thinking creatively about what the church will look like in three to five years.
4. Divide the leaders into groups, and give them questions to investigate. Ask them to report back on their findings in three months. Here are some questions to get them started:
   - Over the next three to five years, how will our church change demographically?
   - Will we have more male or female members?
   - Which age group will grow the fastest? Why?
   - What will the ethnicity, socioeconomic factors, and education of our members be like in three years?
   - How will the neighborhoods around the church look?
   - What developments are planned that we don't know about?
   - Is there a plan for a new Wal-Mart, a shopping mall, or a low-income subsidized apartment complex to buy land near the church?
   - Is there a new highway or off-ramp that will upset the traffic flow?
   - How will traffic flow change based on new construction?
   - Is the local school board considering a new school building?
   - Is the school an elementary, middle, or high school? What does that tell us about growth in this area?
   - Are there water or electrical lines being run to a certain location?

- Has a developer filed plans for a subdivision even though work hasn't begun on the land?

The answers to these questions and others like them can help us to understand how the needs of our members might be changing in the next three to five years.

5. Opportunities are never postponed; they're lost forever. We will miss opportunities if we are not intentionally preparing for them now.

6. Leaders need to spend more time thinking about the future and less time thinking about the past.

7. The one thing we can do about the past is learn from it, but the lessons are valuable only if they are applied to the future.

8. Futuring leaders:
   - Forecast trends, envision scenarios, and help create the desired future.
   - Look through the windshield while they drive, not the rearview mirror.
   - Are vision driven.
   - Say things like, "Where are we going? What are we going to do?" not "Where have we been?"
   - Lead meetings based on what is coming up, rather than what has already happened.
   - Talk with a vocabulary that is about the future.

9. Employees who work for futuring leaders:
   - Deal with projections instead of reports.
   - Spend little time debriefing and much time planning.

10. We can't be futuring leaders alone. We must take time to help our teammates learn to be future gazers and future planners.

11. One of the hardest lessons to learn is that the leaders who got us to this point may not be the ones who carry us to the future.

12. Walt Disney said, "The future is not the result of choices among alternative paths offered in the present—it is a place that is created—created first in the mind and will; created next in activity."[2]

13. As leaders, we need to have our minds on the future and have the activity to back it up.

Notes

1 Dave Kreft, "A Leader and His Vision," www.gospelcom.net/navs/cdm/ld/k2-01.htm.

2 Quoted in S. Richard Fedrizzi, "Iowa Environmental Project Op-Ed," www.iowachild.org/editorials/ed01a.htm.

CHAPTER FIFTEEN

LEGACY

This is the beginning of a new day. You have been given this day to use as you will. You can waste it or use it for good. What you do today is important because you are exchanging a day of your life for it. When tomorrow comes, this day will be gone forever; in its place is something that you have left behind ... let it be something good.

—Author unknown

In the introduction of this book, I talked about a rock that slid down a hill during a mudslide and came to rest in the middle of the road, completely blocking cars from getting around it. I used the example of the rock to help us think about what blocks us. What keeps us from being more successful leaders?

I've identified the fifteen common challenges all leaders face. They are the rocks that block our roads, the challenges that shake our leadership ladder. At different times in our careers, we may feel like we've got one or more of these challenges handled; but they are never completely conquered. The same challenges will continue to reoccur in new and different ways as we grow.

To end this book on the challenge of legacy, then, might seem a little out of place. Isn't legacy something that we leave when we die? How could that be a challenge now? Besides, we really don't have much control over our legacies, do we?

Actually, we don't have to be dead to have a legacy. We are creating it everyday in how we handle the challenges we face. The concept of legacy underlies each one of the fourteen challenges I've already discussed. That's why it is the fifteenth. How we handle each of the previous fourteen challenges is what makes up our legacy.

Specifically, a legacy is dependent on:

- our focus.
- how well we cast vision.
- how we communicate.
- how we make decisions.
- the team we choose.
- the leaders we develop.
- how we handle change.
- how we handle conflict.
- whether we had organizational congruence.
- how we handled money.
- how we allocated our time.
- our ability to delegate.
- our ability to execute plans.
- our planning for the future.

The way we handled these challenges is the legacy we leave after we've moved on, changed jobs, or died. No leader is immune from these challenges. But what is important is how we handle these life and leadership storms. Our choices, our actions, and our behaviors become the legacies we leave the people around us. That's why this is challenge number fifteen. Do our people know that we are here on assignment? Do we know what legacy we will leave? We need to begin our leadership careers with the end in mind. We need to live intentionally in such a way that we pass on our core values.

What the Bible **Says about Legacy**

In John 15:16 Jesus said, "Ye have not chosen me, but I have chosen you, and ordained you, that ye should go and bring forth fruit, and that your fruit should remain: that whatsoever ye shall ask of the Father in my name, he may give it you" (KJV).

There are three parts to this verse, and they are all relevant to our lives and legacies. The first part is the past; that's God's part. He says that he has chosen us and ordained us. That is something he did, and we can't do anything about it but accept it gratefully.

In the next section, he says that we should go forth and bear fruit. This is something active; this is the part we have control over. Many of us fulfill this mandate in the work we do. We build new facilities, we start new programs, and we grow existing ministries. We work hard doing our part, and we're excited and blessed by the fruit that we see as a result.

In the last part of the verse, Jesus promises that whatever we ask in the name of the Father, the Father will give to us. But there is a condition on this promise. Right before the promise Jesus tells us to bring forth fruit, and that our fruit should *remain,* then whatever we ask in his name will be given to us. I think we often fail to catch that middle part. It isn't that we're to bring forth any kind of fruit; we're to bring forth the kind of fruit that will remain. So the real question is: What are we doing to make sure that our fruit remains?

I've told pastors of huge churches, "This is a great campus full of wonderful facilities, but one day it will go away." Buildings will burn. Programs and ministries can change as quickly as the leaders change. Church vans and church buses, TV and radio programs, they will also come and go. So what will remain? If we died today, what have we done that will remain?

I believe that the only thing that truly remains is the *who,* never the *what.* That's why it is important for us as leaders not to get caught up in the what that surrounds us. We need to invest in the people. Those people might be the members of our churches who benefit from the what (programs and buildings). Those people might also be the leaders we've developed who will bring forth their own fruit. We have to make up our minds that our legacies will not be about buildings, marquees, or TV programs.

Yes, we are doing good work bringing forth fruit. We should celebrate that. But to bring forth fruit that remains, we have to

> **Only people, never things, can be our legacies.**

invest in other people. That doesn't mean we stop all our labors. Instead, it means that we focus more attention on the ones who remain. Our legacies should be about other people. What are we doing to intentionally invest in others? How do we make sure that our legacies remain in them and that their legacies go on to remain in others?

Once we find the thing that remains and start pouring ourselves into it, not only does that action define our legacies, but, according to the verse, it means that God will start answering our prayers. Whatever we ask in his name he will give to us. Only people, never things, can be our legacies.

The Legacy **Challenge**

There are recurring themes in this book: the importance of focus, strategic planning, and living intentionally. We've talked about when to concentrate on the *who* and when to focus on the *what*. We've also discussed the difference between abstract and concrete communication. All of these topics come together under legacy. We don't want an abstract legacy.

We want to have a concrete legacy. Rather than, "He was a good man," we want people to say, "He gave his lunch to a hungry child." Rather than "he was a good leader," we want to hear,

"He invested in me." After we've changed jobs, moved on to new challenges, or gone to join the Lord, we want others to remember us specifically and concretely.

I've also warned that many of these fifteen challenges will come up repeatedly in our leadership careers in new ways and different forms. But in an effort to help us focus on our legacies, on the fruit we want to remain, I've included an intentionality worksheet that can help us to consider how we want our legacies reflected in each of these challenges.

Consider the ideas that have been presented about each challenge, then focusing on the end, take a minute to write down how each one should be handled. For example, under conflict maybe you would write, "When challenged by conflict I intend to face it head on and ensure that regardless of the outcome both parties are healthy."

Under execution you might write, "When challenged by execution on the part of my team, I will pay more attention to make sure that I clearly and concretely communicate my expectations."

The point of this exercise is to take the things I've written about and begin intentionally living them. Having a strategic plan for our legacies helps us to surmount each challenge in a way that will remain after we're gone.

Intentionality Worksheet

1. When challenged by focus, I intend to _____
   _____
   _____

2. When challenged by vision casting, I intend to _____
   _____
   _____

3. When challenged by communication, I intend to _____
   _____
   _____

4. When challenged by decision making, I intend to ____
   _____
   _____

5. When challenged by choosing my team, I intend to __
   _____
   _____

6. When challenged by leadership development, I intend
   to _____
   _____

7. When challenged by change and transition, I intend to
   _____
   _____

8. When challenged by conflict, I intend to _____
   _____
   _____

9. When challenged by organizational congruence, I intend to _____

_____

10. When challenged by financial management, I intend to

_____

_____

11. When challenged by time allocation, I intend to _____

_____

_____

12. When challenged by control and delegation, I intend to

_____

_____

13. When challenged by execution, I intend to _____

_____

_____

14. When challenged by future thinking, I intend to _____

_____

_____

15. I intend for my legacy to be _____

_____

_____

John 17:4 says, "I have glorified thee on the earth: I have finished the work which thou gavest me to do" (KJV). The same verse in *The Message* says, "I glorified you on earth by completing down to the last detail what you assigned me to do." That is my hope. There is no better way for us to finish than to complete to the last detail what we've been assigned and have our fruit remain.

> I have glorified thee on the earth:
> I have finished the work which
> thou gavest me to do.
> -John 17:4

Teaching Points

1. No leader is immune from the challenges discussed. The same challenges will continue to reoccur in new and different ways as we grow.

2. Our legacies are created by how we handle the challenges we face. Our choices, our actions, and our behaviors become the legacies we leave.

3. We need to begin our leadership careers with the end in mind. We need to live intentionally in such a way that we pass on our core values.

4. Consider this verse: "Ye have not chosen me, but I have chosen you, and ordained you, that ye should go and bring forth fruit, and that your fruit should remain: that whatsoever ye shall ask of the Father in my name, he may give it you" (John 15:16, KJV).

   • The first part of the verse is the past; that's God's part.

   • In the middle part, Jesus says that we should go forth and bear fruit. This is something active; this is the part we have control over.

   • In the last part of the verse, Jesus promises that whatever we ask in the name of the Father, the Father will give to us, conditioned on bringing forth fruit that remains.

- So the real question is: What are we doing to make sure that our fruit remains?

5. The only thing that truly remains is the who, never the what.

6. It is important for us as leaders not to get caught up in the what that surrounds us. We need to invest in people.

    - What are we doing to intentionally invest in others?

    - How do we make sure that our legacies remain in them and that their legacies go on to remain in others?

7. Only people, never things can be our legacy.

8. Having a strategic plan for our legacies can help us to surmount each challenge in a way that will remain after we're gone.

9. John 17:4 says, "I glorified you on earth by completing down to the last detail what you assigned me to do" (MSG). There is no better way for us to finish than to complete to the last detail what God has assigned us and have it remain.

About Dr. Samuel R. Chand

As a *Dream Releaser*, Sam Chand serves pastors, ministries, and businesses as a leadership architect and change strategist. He is a popular and much sought after speaker for churches, corporations, leadership and ministry conferences, and other leadership development seminars.

In 1973, while a student at Beulah Heights Bible College, Sam Chand served as janitor, cook, and dishwasher. He graduated and was ordained in the ministry in 1977 and went on to serve as an associate and senior pastor in several churches. Sixteen years later, he returned to BHBC to serve as the president for the next 14 years. Under his leadership, BHBC became one of the fastest growing bible colleges in America experiencing a 600% increase in student growth, an enrollment of approximately 700 students from over 400 churches, 45 denominations, and 32 countries. Beulah Heights Bible College is also the country's largest predominantly African-American bible college. He currently serves the school as Chancellor.

Currently, Dr. Chand ...

- Consults with businesses and large churches on leadership and capacity enhancing issues
- Conducts nation-wide leadership conferences
- Presents at international leadership conferences with Dr. John Maxwell's ministry of EQUIP
- Serves on the board of EQUIP, with the goal to equip one million leaders world-wide
- Oversees and leads Bishop Eddie L. Long's leadership development initiatives through Father's House, Spirit & Truth and other leadership development events
- Is on the Board of Faith Academy, an accredited Christian school

- Works as a facilitator of African-American Consortium of Theological Studies (AACTS), a ministry in Kenya to bring collaboration and leadership development to bear upon major churches, denominations and government in Kenya
- Dr. Chand has authored and published five books, which are used worldwide for leadership development. His books include:

> *What's Shakin' Your Ladder: 15 Challenges All Leaders Face* advice for leaders on how to overcome the things that are blocking them.
>
> *Who Moved Your Ladder: Your Next Bold Move* This book provides pragmatic guidelines for dealing with transitions in life and leadership.
>
> *Who's Holding Your Ladder* A reminder to that the most critical decision leaders will make is selecting who will be on their leadership team.
>
> *FUTURING: Leading your Church into Tomorrow* This book is helps leaders to begin a future oriented dialog about their organization.
>
> *Failure: The Womb of Success* a compilation of stories on how to overcome failure with contributions from twenty respected Christian leaders.

Chand's educational background includes an honorary Doctor of Divinity from Heritage Bible College, a Master of Arts in Biblical Counseling from Grace Theological Seminary, a Bachelor of Arts in Biblical Education from Beulah Heights Bible College and a BA - I (one) from Lucknow University, India.

Dr. Chand shares his life and love with his wife Brenda, two daughters Rachel and Deborah and granddaughter Adeline.

Being raised in a pastor's home in India has uniquely equipped Dr. Chand to share his passion – that of mentoring, developing and inspiring leaders to break all limits—in ministry and the marketplace.

For further information please contact:

Samuel R. Chand Ministries, Inc.
P.O. Box 18145, Atlanta, GA 30316
(404) 627-2681 Ext. 108
www.samchand.com
samuel.chand@beulah.org

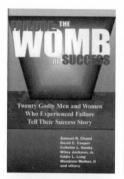

FAILURE:
The Womb of Success

Twenty Godly Men and Women Who experienced Failure Tell Their Success Story

FUTURING:
Leading Your Church into Tomorrow

The message will never change. But the methods to present the message can and must change to reach a realm of churchgoers. Forty-four specific areas that are changing in the church today.

WHO'S HOLDING YOUR LADDER?
Leadership's Most Critical Decision— Selecting Your Leaders

Those around you, not you, the visionary, will determine your success.

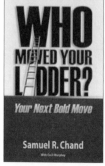

WHO MOVED YOUR LADDER?
Your Next Bold Move

Guidelines for dealing with transitions in life and leadership.

HOW TO ORDER LEADERSHIP
RESOURCES BY SAMUEL R. CHAND

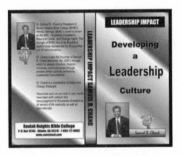

CD
$ 20 EACH

Developing a Leadership Culture

- Why do leaders do what they do?
- Why and when leaders make changes?
- Vision levels of people
- Contemporary leadership
- Why leaders fail
- Qualities of a successful leader

Understanding People:

Managing Conflicts in Your Ministry

- What conflict does
- High maintenance relationships
- Predictable times of conflict
- Levels of conflict
- Diffusing conflict
- Resolving conflict

Formation of a Leader

- Spiritual Formation:
  You were born to lead—be secure
- Skill Formation:
  Lessons on how Moses became a leader
- Strategic Formation: Live the life you were
  meant to live while investing your life in others—
  your legacy

Who's Holding Your Ladder?

- Ladder holders determine the leader's ascent
- Selecting your ladder holders
- Different ladder holders for different levels
- Qualities of a good ladder holder
- Development of ladder holders
- Leaders versus Managers
- Turning ladder holders into ladder climbers

**CD
$ 20 EACH**

CHANGE:
Leading Change Effectively

- Healthy confessions for those leading change
- Tradition and traditionalism
- Responding to seasons and times
- Levels of change
- Factors that facilitate or hinder change
- Steps for positive change
- Selling your idea
- Creating a team
- Personal challenges of the leader leading change

**BOOK
$ 15 EACH**

**CD
$ 20 EACH**

FUTURING:
Leading Your Church Into Tomorrow

- Futuring leadership traits
- Challenges for the 21st century
- How ministry will change in the next 3-7 years
- Motivational fuels for 21st century church
- Addition versus multiplication of leaders

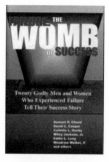

FAILURE:
The Womb of Success

- Failure is an event not a person
- Failure is never final
- Twenty leaders tell their stories

NOTES

1. BULK purchase (10 or more) rates available.
2. Credit cards & checks accepted

CALL

Toll Free 1-888-777-2422
Jeffery Gray at Extension 108

WRITE

Samuel R. Chand Ministries
P.O. Box 18145
Atlanta, GA 30316

WEBSITE

www.samchand.com

EMAIL

samuel.chand@beulah.org

NOTES

NOTES